YOUR PERSONAL
HOROSCOPE
2019

GEMINI

GW00418166

YOUR PERSONAL HOROSCOPE 2019

GEMINI

22nd May–21st June

igloobooks

Published in 2018
by Igloo Books Ltd
Cottage Farm
Sywell
NN6 0BJ
www.igloobooks.com

Produced for Igloo Books by Foulsham Publishing Ltd, The Old Barrel Store,
Drayman's Lane, Marlow, Bucks SL7 2FF, England

FIR003 0718
2 4 6 8 10 9 7 5 3 1
ISBN: 978-1-78810-532-3

This is an abridged version of material originally published
in Old Moore's Horoscope and Astral Diary.

Cover designed by Nicholas Gage
Edited by Bobby Newlyn-Jones

Printed and manufactured in China

CONTENTS

CONTENTS

INTRODUCTION

Your personal horoscopes have been specifically created to allow you to get the most from astrological patterns and the way they have a bearing on not only your zodiac sign, but nuances within it. Using the diary section of the book you can read about the influences and possibilities of each and every day of the year. It will be possible for you to see when you are likely to be cheerful and happy, or those times when your nature is in retreat and you will be more circumspect. The diary will help to give you a feel for the specific 'cycles' of astrology and the way they can subtly change your day-to-day life. For example, when you see the sign ☿, this means that the planet Mercury is retrograde at that time. Retrograde means it appears to be running backwards through the zodiac. Such a happening has a significant effect on communication skills, but this is only one small aspect of how the personal horoscope can help you.

With your personal horoscope, the story doesn't end with the diary pages. It includes simple ways for you to work out the zodiac sign the Moon occupied at the time of your birth, and what this means for your personality. In addition, if you know the time of day you were born, it is possible to discover your Ascendant, yet another important guide to your personal make-up and potential.

Many readers are interested in relationships and in knowing how well they get on with people of other astrological signs. You might also be interested in the way you appear to very different sorts of individuals. If you are such a person, the section on Venus will be of particular interest. Despite the rapidly changing position of this planet, you can work out your Venus sign, and learn what bearing it will have on your life.

Using your personal horoscope you can travel on one of the most fascinating and rewarding journeys that anyone can take – the journey to a better realisation of self.

THE ESSENCE OF GEMINI

Exploring the Personality of Gemini the Twins

(22ND MAY – 21ST JUNE)

What's in a sign?

When working at your best there isn't much doubt that you are one of the most popular people to be found anywhere in the zodiac. Why? Because you are bubbly, charming, full of fun and the perfect companion. But there's more to it than that. Your natural mercurial charm could coax the birds down from the trees and you exude the sort of self-confidence that would convince almost anyone that you know exactly what you want, and how to go about getting it. Virtually any task you choose to undertake is done in a flash and when at your best you can remove more obstacles than a bulldozer.

So, you ask, if all this is true, why aren't I doing even better in life than I am? The simple fact is that beneath all the bravado and that oh-so-confident exterior is a small child, who is often lost and afraid in a world that can be complicated, large and threatening. If ever there was a person who epitomised a split personality, it surely has to be the typical Gemini subject. That impulsive, driving, Mercury-ruled enthusiasm simply insists on pushing you to the front of any queue, but once you are there the expectations of all those standing behind can begin to prey on your mind. This is why so many of your plans stall before they are brought to completion, and it also explains all those times that you simply ran out of energy and virtually collapsed into a heap. There is a lot to learn if you want to get the best out of what the zodiac has given you. Fortunately, life itself is your schoolyard and there is plenty you can do to make the very best of your natural talents.

Read through the following sections carefully and when you have done so, get ready to put all your latent talents to the test. As you grow in confidence, you will find that you are not as alone as you sometimes think. The keywords for the sign of Gemini are

'I think', but for you this isn't an insular process. Life itself is your launching pad to success and happiness – just as long as you learn to concentrate on the task at hand.

Gemini resources

The part of the zodiac occupied by the sign of Gemini, has, for many centuries, been recognised as the home of communication. Almost everything that you are as an individual is associated with your need to keep in constant touch with the world at large. This trait is so marked that Geminis seem to dream more than most other people, so that even in your sleep the need to keep looking, talking and explaining is as essential to you as breathing.

What might be slightly less well understood regarding the sign of the Twins is that you are a natural listener, too. One of the reasons for your popularity is that you always seem interested in what those around you have to say. And beneath this desire to know is a latent ability to understand much about your friends and relatives at an almost instinctive level. Gemini individuals can keep moving forward, even against heavy odds, just as long as a particular project or task feels right, and you should never underestimate the power of your instincts.

The level of your energy, and the way you project it into everything you do, can be inclined to leave others breathless. This is one of your secrets of success because you can be at the winning post so often, whilst others are still putting on their shoes. You are not a trend follower, but rather a trendsetter and no matter if you are on the dance floor of a trendy club, or on a senior citizens' trip to the coast, you are likely to be the centre of attention. The enterprising, interesting Gemini skips through life like a barefoot child and elicits just as much joy from those who prefer to stand and watch.

Beneath the happy-go-lucky exterior is a great deal more savvy than many astrologers were once willing to grant to the sign of the Twins. However, the advent of the multimedia age has brought Gemini into a society that it not only understands, but in which it excels. On the telephone, the computer and especially the Internet, you spread your sense of fun and offer everyone you meet an invigorating dose of your enthusiasm, knowledge and zest for life.

Beneath the surface

It is likely that most Gemini individuals would consider themselves to be uncomplicated and easy to understand. 'What you see is what you get' seems to be a statement made extremely often by those born under this zodiac sign. It isn't at all true. On the contrary, the Gemini nature is multi- faceted, cranky and often obscure. In short, you have more skins than a Spanish onion. If Geminis have often been referred to as 'superficial' or 'shallow' they probably only have themselves to blame, since they are the first to describe themselves this way. But the truth is that you are a deep thinker – in fact one of the deepest of all. The only reason you don't consider yourself in this light is that your thought processes, like your speech, are lightning fast.

Because of its chatterbox ways, Gemini is often a very misunderstood zodiac sign. But listen to yourself talking. Many of the statements you make to those around you will be ended in questions such as 'Don't you think?'. Why should this be so? Well the fact is that you are never so certain of yourself as you want to give the impression of being and as a result you invariably seek the confirmation of the world at large that your ideas and plans are sound. If the response you want is late, or not forthcoming at all, you tend to feel insecure and start to fidget. In time, this leads to worrying – the worst possible state for the Gemini mind. The dividing line between mental and physical is not at all well defined in your case, so you will often seem most fatigued at those times when you are less than sure of your direction in life.

You almost always start out with the right intentions and would never deliberately hurt another individual. To your very core you are generous and kind. Unfortunately, in a busy schedule there isn't always time to let your sensitivity show, and especially not when you live your life constantly in the fast lane. It is almost instinctive for Geminis to divide their lives into 'the job I am doing now', 'the task I will be undertaking in a few minutes' and 'the things I am planning for later'. But even your mind is only capable of so much, so it's essential that you find moments to stop the whirl and buzz of your innermost thoughts. To do so is the hardest task you will undertake, but it's the surest path to health and success that you can ever choose.

Making the best of yourself

It is quite clear that you were never cut out to be a monk or a nun, or at least not of the contemplative sort. Mental desert islands are a natural torture chamber to your zodiac sign and so it's obvious, right from the start, that you need other people just as much as plants need rain. On the other hand, you also need to stop thinking that you can be in control of everything. The hardest lesson for any Gemini to learn is to be selective. Gemini sees life like a wonderfully prepared buffet at which every successive dish offers something absolutely delicious. The idea of trying some of the treats later simply doesn't occur and at the level of daily life, the result can often be mental indigestion. Concentration is the key, though without losing the essential freshness and appeal that is the hallmark of your natural personality. 'One job at a time' is the best adage, but it doesn't come easily for you.

Your natural talents are suited to intellectual browsing, so you are definitely at your best where flexibility is present. The chances are that you don't really enjoy getting your hands dirty, but even this doesn't really matter as long as you are learning something on the way. You revel in absorbing responsibility and tend to think on your feet. Travel is important to you, not only because it broadens your mind, but also because you are naturally good at languages. You possess a very human touch; you are not frightened to show your emotions and work well alongside others. However, you might function even better if you maintained confidence in your decisions and tried rather less than you sometimes do to be popular with everyone. This comes easier when you are dealing with a subject matter that you fully understand, and that in turn takes concentration, which you can only cultivate with practice.

The impressions you give

This section may appeal the most to Gemini subjects because you care deeply about the opinions others have of you. To a certain extent, everything you do in a public sense is a sort of performance and, just like an actor, you are interested in what the critics have to say. To a great extent you can relax, because there's a good chance that you are much loved. How could it be otherwise? You spread sunshine wherever you go, though it has to be said that you can promote a good deal of confusion, too, on occasions.

You have to be prepared to take on board the fact that some people will like you more than others do. This is a natural consequence of being such an upfront person. There are people who swim around in the sea of life without making so much as a ripple, but you are definitely not one of them. Some of the individuals you meet will simply not be turned on by the gregarious, enthusiastic, go-getting creature that you are. Once you understand this fact, and stop trying to force your attentions in the wrong direction, your life will be happier as a result.

Another way you can help yourself is to cultivate humility. Gemini people know at least something about almost everything, but there is truth in the adage that 'a little knowledge can be a dangerous thing'. The most successful of those born under the sign of the Twins have learned to defer to experts, most of whom don't take kindly to criticism. You can still maintain your own opinions, but a quiet self-assurance will win you more friends than forcing half-formed opinions on the world at large. On the whole though, you can relax because you are almost certainly more popular than you think you are.

The way forward

Age matters less to Gemini than it does to any other zodiac sign. The fact is that you are always young in your head, no matter how much some of your joints might creak. But even in a physical sense it is important to look after yourself and to recognise those areas that need the most attention. Gemini rules the chest, and especially the lungs, so you should never be a smoker. The sign is also related to the general nervous system, which is almost always pushed to the edge in your frantic attempts to get just as much out of life as possible. Relaxation is just as important as physical exercise, and since you naturally love words, reading is as good as anything. All the same, you shouldn't be constantly trying to learn something, and need to understand that entertainment for its own sake is often enough for your busy brain.

No matter how much your mind wanders, you need to be master of at least one subject – this is the way to success in a professional sense. Whatever your job (and Gemini people are rarely out of work) you will nearly always find yourself in charge of others. Use all the natural understanding that lies at the centre of your being to understand how others tick and you are almost certain to prosper.

On the way through life, professional or social, you can't avoid dealing in gossip, because this is an essential part of the way you function. Casual contacts are inevitable, so you may have hundreds of acquaintances but only a few very close personal friends. However, when you do find yourself absolutely on the same wavelength as another individual, it can be the most enlightening experience imaginable. Geminis often find themselves involved in more than one deep, romantic attachment in their lives, though this is far less likely if your partner is also your best friend.

Don't give in to self-doubt, but at the same time avoid giving the impression that you know everything. Cultivate patience and spend at least a few minutes each day doing absolutely nothing. Overall, balance is essential, and that isn't always easy to achieve when tottering along the tightrope of life. All the same, a Gemini who is at ease with him or herself excels socially and grows wiser with each passing day.

GEMINI ON THE CUSP

Astrological profiles are altered for those people born at either the beginning or the end of a zodiac sign, or, more properly, on the 'cusp' of a sign. In the case of Gemini this would be on the 22nd of May and for two or three days after, and similarly at the end of the sign, probably from the 19th to the 21st of June.

The Taurus Cusp – 22nd May to 25th May

It would be fair to suggest that Gemini tends to predominate over almost any zodiac sign with which it is associated so, the trends of this most capricious and gregarious sign tend to show out well at both cusps. Heavily affected by Taurus, however, you are likely to be steadier and more willing to take your time over important matters. Staying power is better and the Taurean cusp inspires a quiet confidence on occasions that seems to contrast sharply with the more chatty qualities of the Twins. Entrenched attitudes are certainly more likely, with a need to prove a point and to seek objectives through determined effort. Taurus, here, does little to stem the generally cheerful qualities of Gemini, but there is likely a more serious side to your nature and a willingness to exhibit the sort of patience that is often lacking in the Sun sign of Gemini.

In matters of love, you are more likely than most Geminis to show a high degree of constancy, even if settling on a partner is a longer process in your case. You can't be detached from relationships in the way that a dyed-in-the-wool Gemini can and it's important for you to know that you are loved. Professionally speaking, you have much going for you because in addition to the 'get ahead at any cost' quality that comes from the direction of the Twins, you are persevering, honourable, steadfast and reliable. It is probably in matters of business that the most positive qualities of this astrological matching are to be seen.

Health matters are also stabilised to a greater extent on this cusp, partly because the nature is not half as nervy, and more care is taken to get the level of rest and relaxation that is just as important to Gemini. Less rush and push is evident, though a need for change and diversity probably won't be eradicated from your basic nature. There is a good chance that you are something of a home bird, at least most of the time, and family matters are often paramount in your mind. Probably the most noticeable trait is your tendency to be more tidy than the orthodox Gemini – which some would say is no bad thing.

The Cancer Cusp – 19th June to 21st June

It can be argued that the gradual slip from the sign of Gemini to that of Cancer is slightly less well defined than is the case for Taurus and Gemini. However, when working as stereotypes, Gemini and Cancer are radically different sorts of signs. Gemini seeks to intellectualise everything, so its catch phrase is 'I think', while Cancer's is 'I feel'. What we would therefore expect, in this case, is a gradually quieter and less fickle nature as the Sun climbs closer to Cancer. You are likely to show more genuine consideration for other people. Actually this is something of a misnomer because Gemini people are very caring too, it's simply a matter of you showing the tendency more, and you are certainly more tied to home and family than any true Gemini would be. A quiet perseverance typifies your individual nature and you are quite prepared to wait for your objectives to mature, which the Twins are less likely to do. Comfort and security are important to you, though, apparently paradoxically, you are a great traveller and love to see fresh fields and pastures new. Given the opportunity you could even find yourself living in some far, distant land.

In affairs of the heart, you are clearly more steadfast than Gemini and love to be loved. The difference here is that Gemini wants to be liked by everyone, but will quickly move on in cases where this proves to be difficult. You, on the other hand, would take any sort of rebuff as a personal insult and would work hard to reverse the situation. Confidence may not be your middle name, but you are supported by the Gemini ability to bluff your way through when necessary, even if the motivation is of a more consistent nature.

You may well be a person who has to rest in order to recharge batteries that sometimes run quite low. Your nervous system may not be all that strong on occasions and this fact could manifest itself in the form of stomach troubles of one sort or another. Common sense counts when it comes to looking after yourself and that's something that the sign of Cancer does possess. Whether you are truly satisfied with yourself, your own efforts may sometimes be in some doubt.

GEMINI AND ITS ASCENDANTS

The nature of every individual on the planet is composed of the rich variety of zodiac signs and planetary positions that were present at the time of their birth. Your Sun sign, which in your case is Gemini, is one of the many factors when it comes to assessing the unique person you are. Probably the most important consideration, other than your Sun sign, is to establish the zodiac sign that was rising over the eastern horizon at the time that you were born. This is your Ascending or Rising sign. Most popular astrology fails to take account of the Ascendant, and yet its importance remains with you from the very moment of your birth, through every day of your life. The Ascendant is evident in the way you approach the world, and so, when meeting a person for the first time, it is this astrological influence that you are most likely to notice first. Our Ascending sign essentially represents what we appear to be, while the Sun sign is what we feel inside ourselves.

The Ascendant also has the potential for modifying our overall nature. For example, if you were born at a time of day when Gemini was passing over the eastern horizon (this would be around the time of dawn) then you would be classed as a double Gemini. As such, you would typify this zodiac sign, both internally and in your dealings with others. However, if your Ascendant sign turned out to be a Water sign, such as Pisces, there would be a profound alteration of nature, away from the expected qualities of Gemini.

One of the reasons why popular astrology often ignores the Ascendant is that it has always been rather difficult to establish. We have found a way to make this possible by devising an easy-to-use table, which you will find on page 157 of this book. Using this, you can establish your Ascendant sign at a glance. You will need to know your rough time of birth, then it is simply a case of following the instructions.

For those readers who have no idea of their time of birth it might be worth allowing a good friend, or perhaps your partner, to read through the section that follows this introduction. Someone who deals with you on a regular basis may easily discover your Ascending sign, even though you could have some difficulty establishing it for yourself. A good understanding of this component of your nature is essential if you want to be aware of that 'other person' who is responsible for the way you make contact with the world at large. Your Sun sign, Ascendant sign, and the other pointers in this book will, together, allow you a far better understanding of what makes you tick as an individual. Peeling back the different layers of your astrological make-up can be an enlightening experience, and the Ascendant may represent one of the most important layers of all.

Gemini with Gemini Ascendant

You are one of the most fun-loving characters in the zodiac, with a great sense of humour and the ability to sell refrigerators to Eskimos. Most people would think that you have nerves of steel and that there is nothing that lies beyond the scope of your ready wit and silver tongue. Unfortunately, it isn't quite as simple as this because you bruise easily, especially when you discover that someone is not as fond of you as they might be. Routines get on your nerves and you need as much change and diversity as life will allow. You are the life and soul of any party that is going on in your vicinity, and you have the ability to mix business and pleasure, so should get on well as a result.

In love you tend to be rather fickle and the double Gemini is inclined to jump from relationship to relationship in pursuit of something that remains rather difficult to define. There are occasions when your life lacks stability and this can be provided by the right sort of personal attachment, assuming you manage to find it eventually. It is clear that you are not the easiest person to understand, even though you probably think that you do not have a complicated bone in your body. Most important of all, you have many, many friends and this will be the case all your life.

Gemini with Cancer Ascendant

Many astrologers would say that this is a happy combination because some of the more flighty qualities of Gemini are somewhat modified by the steady influence of Cancer the Crab. To all intents and purposes you show the friendly and gregarious qualities of Gemini, but there is a thoughtful and even sometimes a serious quality that would not be present in the double Gemini example, left. Looking after people is high on your list of priorities and you do this most of the time. This is made possible because you have greater staying power than Gemini is usually said to possess and you can see fairly complicated situations through to their conclusion without becoming bored on the way.

The chances are that you will have many friends and that these people show great concern for your well-being, because you choose them carefully and show them a great deal of consideration. However, you will still be on the receiving end of gossip on occasions, and need to treat such situations with a healthy pinch of salt. Like all Geminis, your nervous system is not as strong as you would wish to believe and family pressures in particular can put great strain on you. Activities of all kinds take your fancy and many people with this combination are attracted to sailing or wind surfing.

Gemini with Leo Ascendant

Many Gemini people think about doing great things, whilst those who enjoy a Leo Ascendant do much more than simply think. You are the truly intrepid Gemini, but you always keep a sense of humour and are especially good to be around. Bold and quite fearless, you are inclined to go where nobody has gone before, no matter if this is into a precarious business venture or up a mountain that has not been previously climbed. It is people such as you who first explored the world and you love to know what lies around the next corner and over the far hill.

Kind and loving, you are especially loyal to your friends and would do almost anything on their behalf. As a result they show the greatest concern for you, too. However, there are times when the cat walks alone and you are probably better at being on your own than would often be the case for the typical Gemini subject. In many ways you are fairly self-contained and don't tend to get bored too much unless you are forced to do the same things time and time again. You have a great sense of fun, can talk to anyone and usually greet the world with a big smile.

Gemini with Virgo Ascendant

A Virgo Ascendant means that you are ruled by Mercury, both through your Sun sign and through the sign that was rising at the time of your birth. This means that words are your basic tools in life and you use them to the full. Some writers have this combination because even speaking to people virtually all the time is not enough. Although you have many friends, you are fairly high-minded which means that you can make enemies too. The fact is that people either care very much for you, or else they don't like you at all. This can be difficult for you to come to terms with because you don't really set out to cause friction – it often simply attracts itself to you.

Although you love to travel, home is important too. There is a basic insecurity in your nature that comes about as a result of an overdose of Mercury, which makes you nervy and sometimes far less confident than anyone would guess. Success in your life may be slower arriving with this combination because you are determined to achieve your objectives on your own terms and this can take time. Always a contradiction, often a puzzle to others, your ultimate happiness in life is directly proportional to the effort you put in, though this should not mean wearing yourself out on the way.

Gemini with Libra Ascendant

What a happy-go-lucky soul you are, and how popular you tend to be with those around you! Libra is, like Gemini, an Air sign and this means that you are the communicator par excellence, even by Gemini standards. It can sometimes be difficult for you to make up your mind about things because Libra does not exactly aid this process, and especially not when it is allied to mercurial Gemini. Frequent periods of deep thought are necessary and meditation would do you a great deal of good. All the same, although you might sometimes be rather unsure of yourself, you are rarely without a certain balance. Clean and tidy surroundings suit you the best, though this is far from easy to achieve because you are invariably dashing off to some place or other, so you really need someone to sort things out in your absence.

The most important fact of all is that you are much loved by your friends, of which there are likely to be very many. Because you are so willing to help them out, in return they are usually there when it matters and they would go to almost any length on your behalf. You exhibit a fine sense of justice and will usually back those in trouble. Charities tend to be attractive to you and you do much on behalf of those who live on the fringes of society or people who are truly alone.

Gemini with Scorpio Ascendant

What you are and what you appear to be can be two entirely different things with this combination. Although you appear to be every bit as chatty and even as flighty as Gemini tends to be, nothing could be further from the truth. In reality you have many deep and penetrating insights, all of which are geared towards sorting out potential problems before they come along. Few people would have the ability to pull the wool over your eyes and you show a much more astute face to the world than is often the case for Gemini taken on its own. The level of your confidence, although not earth-shattering, is much greater with this combination, and you will not be thwarted once you had made up your mind.

There is a slight danger here, however, because Gemini is always inclined to take problems of one sort or another to heart. In the main these are slight and fleeting, though the presence of Scorpio can intensify reactions and heighten the possibility of depression, which would not be at all fortunate. The best way round this potential problem is to have a wealth of friends, plenty to do and the sort of variety in your life that suits your Mercury ruler. Financial success is not too difficult to achieve with this combination, mainly because you can easily earn money and you have a natural ability to hold on to it.

Gemini with Sagittarius Ascendant

'Tomorrow is another day!' This is your belief and you stick to it. There isn't a brighter or more optimistic soul to be found than you and almost everyone you come into contact with is touched by this fact. Dashing about from one place to another, you manage to get more things done in one day than most other people would achieve in a week. Of course this explains why you are so likely to wear yourself out, and it means that frequent periods of absolute rest are necessary if you are to remain truly healthy and happy. Sagittarius makes you brave and sometimes a little headstrong, so you need to curb your natural enthusiasms now and again, whilst you stop to think about the consequences of some of your actions.

It's not really certain if you do 'think' in the accepted sense of the word, because the lightning qualities of both these signs mean that your reactions are second to none. However, you are not indestructible and you put far more pressure on yourself than would often be sensible. Routines are not your thing at all and many of you manage to hold down two or more jobs at once. It might be an idea to stop and smell the flowers on the way, and you could certainly do with putting your feet up much more than you do. However, you probably won't have read this far into the passage because you will almost certainly have something far more important to do!

Gemini with Capricorn Ascendant

A much more careful and considered combination is evident here. You still have the friendly and chatty qualities of Gemini, though you also possess an astute, clever and deep-thinking quality which can really add bite to the mercurial aspects of your nature. Although you rarely seem to take yourself, or anyone else, all that seriously, in reality you are not easily fooled and usually know the direction in which you are heading. The practical application of your thought processes matter to you and you always give of your best, especially in any professional situation. This combination provides the very best business mind that any Gemini could have and, unlike other versions of the sign, you are willing to allow matters to mature. This quality cannot be overstated, and leads to a form of ultimate achievement that many other Geminis would only guess at.

Family matters are important to you and your home is a special place of retreat, even though you are also willing to get out and meet the world, which is the prerogative of all Gemini types. There are times when you genuinely wish to remain quiet, and when such times arise you may need to explain the situation to some of the bemused people surrounding you. Above all you look towards material gain, without ever losing your sense of humour.

Gemini with Aquarius Ascendant

If you were around in the 1960s there is every chance that you were the first to go around with flowers in your hair. You are unconventional, original, quirky and entertaining. Few people would fail to notice your presence and you take life as it comes, even though on most occasions you are firmly in the driving seat. In all probability you care very much about the planet on which you live and the people with whom you share it. Not everyone understands you, but that does not really matter, for you have more than enough communication skills to put your message across intact. You should avoid wearing yourself out by worrying about things that you cannot control and you would definitely gain from taking time out to meditate. However, whether or not you allow yourself that luxury remains to be seen.

If you are not the most communicative form of Gemini, then you must come a close second. Despite this fact, much of what you have to say makes real sense and you revel in the company of interesting, intelligent and stimulating people, whose opinions on a host of matters will add to your own considerations. You are a true original in every sense of the word and the mere fact of your presence in the world is bound to add to the enjoyment of life, experienced by the many people with whom you make contact each and every day.

Gemini with Pisces Ascendant

There is great duality inherent with this combination and sometimes this can cause a few problems. Part of the trouble stems from the fact that you often fail to realise what you want from life and you could also be accused of failing to take the time out to think things through carefully enough. You are reactive, and although you have every bit of the natural charm that typifies the sign of Gemini, you are more prone to periods of self-doubt and confusion. However, you should not allow these facts to get you down too much because you are also genuinely loved and have a tremendous capacity to look after others, a factor which is more important to you than any other. It's true that personal relationships can sometimes be a cause of difficulty for you, partly because your constant need to know what makes other people tick could drive them up the wall. Accepting people at face value seems to be the best key to happiness of a personal sort and there are occasions when your very real and natural intuition has to be put on hold.

It's likely that you are an original, particularly in the way you dress. An early rebellious stage often gives way to a more comfortable form of eccentricity. When you are at your best just about everyone adores you.

Gemini with Aries Ascendant

This is a fairly jolly combination, though by no means easy for others to come to terms with. You fly about from pillar to post and rarely stop long enough to take a breath. Admittedly this suits your own needs very well, but it can be a source of some disquiet to those around you, since they may not possess your energy or motivation. Those who know you well are deeply in awe of your capacity to keep going long after almost everyone else would have given up and gone home, though this quality is not always wonderful, because it means that you put more pressure on your nervous system than just about any other astrological combination.

You need to be mindful of your nervous system, which responds to the erratic, mercurial quality of a Gemini. Problems only really arise when the Aries part of you makes demands that the Gemini component finds difficult to deal with. There are paradoxes galore here and some of them need sorting out if you are ever fully to understand yourself, or are to be in a position where others know what makes you tick.

In relationships you might be a little fickle, but you are a veritable charmer and never get stuck for the right words, no matter who you are dealing with. Your tenacity knows no bounds, though perhaps sometimes it should!

Gemini with Taurus Ascendant

This is a generally happy combination which finds you better able to externalise the cultured and creative qualities that are inherent in your Taurean side. You love to be around interesting and stimulating people and tend to be just as talkative as the typical Gemini is expected to be. The reason why Gemini helps here is because it lightens the load somewhat. Taurus is not the most introspective sign of the zodiac, but it does have some of that quality, and a Gemini Sun allows you to speak your mind more freely. As a result, you get to know yourself better.

Although your mind tends to be fairly logical, you also enjoy flashes of insight that can cause you to behave in a less rational way from time to time. This is probably no bad thing because life will never be boring with you around. You try to convince yourself that you take on board all the many and varied opinions that come back at you from others, though there is a slight danger of intellectual snobbery if the responses you get are not the expected ones. You particularly like clean houses, funny people and fast cars. Financial rewards can come thick and fast to the Taurus-Ascendant Gemini when the logical, but still inspirational, mind is firmly harnessed to practical matters.

Central with Futures Ascendant

If it generally happens that individuals, their finances being quite uncorrelated to the outlined and relative qualities that are inherent in your finances. Whether to be more careful, adds to accumulate purpose and are apt to take as balances in the typical circumstances. [...] to be [...] the reason why it quite helps [...] to become. If before the [...] character, truth is not the most like pattern. [...] side of the options, but wishes [...] some of the wealth, and a feature can allow to [...] goes you cannot more likely. A useful [...] you get it. I owe you all as [...].

Although your [...] tend to be that beyond, you also enjoy basics or begin they cannot [...] round believe you a lot situation. From time to time. These is probably to feel that, because the will be write being with you in mind. You try to concentrate, much that you affect on, based in the thing and period of opinions that come back as you have others. These is there a shall matter of much, chat numbers on the spaces you are during the expected once. You can estimating the difference many people and feel are financial records. In some field, useful to the thorough knowledge born of what are logical, but still inspirational mind is that, hints back to practical interest.

THE MOON AND THE PART IT PLAYS IN YOUR LIFE

In astrology the Moon is probably the single most important heavenly body after the Sun. Its unique position, as partner to the Earth on its journey around the solar system, means that the Moon appears to pass through the signs of the zodiac extremely quickly. The zodiac position of the Moon at the time of your birth plays a great part in personal character and is especially significant in the build-up of your emotional nature.

Your Own Moon Sign

Discovering the position of the Moon at the time of your birth has always been notoriously difficult because tracking the complex zodiac positions of the Moon is not easy. This process has been reduced to three simple stages with our Lunar Tables. A breakdown of the Moon's zodiac positions can be found from page 35 onwards, so that once you know what your Moon Sign is, you can see what part this plays in the overall build-up of your personal character.

If you follow the instructions on the next page you will soon be able to work out exactly what zodiac sign the Moon occupied on the day that you were born and you can then go on to compare the reading for this position with those of your Sun sign and your Ascendant. It is partly the comparison between these three important positions that goes towards making you the unique individual you are.

How To Discover Your Moon Sign

This is a three-stage process. You may need a pen and a piece of paper, but if you follow the instructions below the process should only take a minute or so.

STAGE 1 First of all you need to know the Moon Age at the time of your birth. If you look at Moon Table 1, on page 33, you will find all the years between 1921 and 2019 down the left side. Find the year of your birth and then trace across to the right to the month of your birth. Where the two intersect you will find a number. This is the date of the New Moon in the month that you were born. You now need to count forward the number of days between the New Moon and your own birthday. For example, if the New Moon in the month of your birth was shown as being the 6th and you were born on the 20th, your Moon Age Day would be 14. If the New Moon in the month of your birth came after your birthday, you need to count forward from the New Moon in the previous month. Whatever the result, jot this number down so that you do not forget it.

STAGE 2 Take a look at Moon Table 2 on page 34. Down the left hand column look for the date of your birth. Now trace across to the month of your birth. Where the two meet you will find a letter. Copy this letter down alongside your Moon Age Day.

STAGE 3 Moon Table 3 on page 34 will supply you with the zodiac sign the Moon occupied on the day of your birth. Look for your Moon Age Day down the left hand column and then for the letter you found in Stage 2. Where the two converge you will find a zodiac sign and this is the sign occupied by the Moon on the day that you were born.

Your Zodiac Moon Sign Explained

You will find a profile of all zodiac Moon Signs on pages 35 to 38, showing in yet another way how astrology helps to make you into the individual that you are. In each daily entry of the Astral Diary you can find the zodiac position of the Moon for every day of the year. This also allows you to discover your lunar birthdays. Since the Moon passes through all the signs of the zodiac in about a month, you can expect something like twelve lunar birthdays each year. At these times you are likely to be emotionally steady and able to make the sort of decisions that have real, lasting value.

MOON TABLE 1

YEAR	APR	MAY	JUN	YEAR	APR	MAY	JUN	YEAR	APR	MAY	JUN
1921	8	7	6	1954	3	2	1/30	1987	28	27	26
1922	27	26	25	1955	22	21	20	1988	16	15	14
1923	16	15	14	1956	11	10	8	1989	6	5	3
1924	4	3	2	1957	29	29	27	1990	25	24	22
1925	23	22	21	1958	19	18	17	1991	13	13	11
1926	12	11	10	1959	8	7	6	1992	3	2	1/30
1927	2	1/30	29	1960	26	26	24	1993	22	21	20
1928	20	19	18	1961	15	14	13	1994	11	10	9
1929	9	9	7	1962	5	4	2	1995	30	29	27
1930	28	28	26	1963	23	23	21	1996	18	18	17
1931	18	17	16	1964	12	11	10	1997	7	6	5
1932	6	5	4	1965	1	1/30	29	1998	26	25	24
1933	24	24	23	1966	20	19	18	1999	16	15	13
1934	13	13	12	1967	9	8	7	2000	4	4	2
1935	3	2	1/30	1968	28	27	26	2001	23	23	21
1936	21	20	19	1969	16	15	14	2002	12	12	10
1937	12	10	8	1970	6	6	4	2003	1	1/30	29
1938	30	29	27	1971	25	24	22	2004	18	16	15
1939	19	19	17	1972	13	13	11	2005	8	8	6
1940	7	7	6	1973	3	2	1/30	2006	27	27	26
1941	26	26	24	1974	22	21	20	2007	17	171	15
1942	15	15	13	1975	11	11	9	2008	6	5	4
1943	4	4	2	1976	29	29	27	2009	26	25	23
1944	22	22	20	1977	18	18	16	2010	14	14	12
1945	12	11	10	1978	7	7	5	2011	3	3	2
1946	2	1/30	29	1979	26	26	24	2012	21	20	19
1947	20	19	18	1980	15	14	13	2013	10	10	8
1948	9	9	7	1981	4	4	2	2014	30	29	27
1949	28	27	26	1982	23	21	20	2015	19	18	17
1950	17	17	15	1983	13	12	11	2016	7	6	4
1951	6	6	4	1984	1	1/30	29	2017	25	25	24
1952	24	23	22	1985	20	19	18	2018	16	15	13
1953	13	13	11	1986	9	8	7	2019	4	3	2

TABLE 2   MOON TABLE 3

DAY	MAY	JUN	M/D	M	N	O	P	Q	R	S
1	M	O	0	TA	GE	GE	GE	CA	CA	CA
2	M	P	1	GE	GE	GE	CA	CA	CA	LE
3	M	P	2	GE	GE	CA	CA	CA	LE	LE
4	M	P	3	GE	CA	CA	CA	LE	LE	LE
5	M	P	4	CA	CA	CA	LE	LE	LE	VI
6	M	P	5	CA	LE	LE	LE	VI	VI	VI
7	M	P	6	LE	LE	LE	VI	VI	VI	LI
8	M	P	7	LE	LE	VI	VI	VI	LI	LI
9	M	P	8	LE	VI	VI	VI	LI	LI	LI
10	M	P	9	VI	VI	VI	LI	LI	SC	SC
11	M	P	10	VI	LI	LI	LI	SC	SC	SC
12	N	Q	11	LI	LI	SC	SC	SC	SA	SA
13	N	Q	12	LI	LI	SC	SC	SA	SA	SA
14	N	Q	13	LI	SC	SC	SC	SA	SA	SA
15	N	Q	14	LI	SC	SC	SA	SA	SA	CP
16	N	Q	15	SC	SA	SA	SA	CP	CP	CP
17	N	Q	16	SC	SA	SA	CP	CP	CP	AQ
18	N	Q	17	SA	SA	CP	CP	CP	AQ	AQ
19	N	Q	18	SA	CP	CP	CP	AQ	AQ	AQ
20	N	Q	19	SA	CP	CP	AQ	AQ	AQ	PI
21	N	Q	20	CP	AQ	AQ	AQ	PI	PI	PI
22	O	R	21	CP	AQ	AQ	PI	PI	PI	AR
23	O	R	22	AQ	AQ	PI	PI	PI	AR	AR
24	O	R	23	AQ	PI	PI	PI	AR	AR	AR
25	O	R	24	AQ	PI	PI	AR	AR	AR	TA
26	O	R	25	PI	AR	AR	AR	TA	TA	TA
27	O	R	26	PI	AR	AR	TA	TA	TA	GE
28	O	R	27	AR	AR	TA	TA	TA	GE	GE
29	O	R	28	AR	TA	TA	TA	GE	GE	GE
30	O	R	29	AR	TA	TA	GE	GE	GE	CA
31	O	–								

AR = Aries, TA = Taurus, GE = Gemini, CA = Cancer, LE = Leo, VI = Virgo,
LI = Libra, SC = Scorpio, SA = Sagittarius, CP = Capricorn, AQ = Aquarius, PI = Pisces

MOON SIGNS

Moon in Aries

You have a strong imagination, courage, determination and a desire to do things in your own way and forge your own path through life.

Originality is a key attribute; you are seldom stuck for ideas although your mind is changeable and you could take the time to focus on individual tasks. Often quick-tempered, you take orders from few people and live life at a fast pace. Avoid health problems by taking regular time out for rest and relaxation.

Emotionally, it is important that you talk to those you are closest to and work out your true feelings. Once you discover that people are there to help, there is less necessity for you to do everything yourself.

Moon in Taurus

The Moon in Taurus gives you a courteous and friendly manner, which means you are likely to have many friends.

The good things in life mean a lot to you, as Taurus is an Earth sign that delights in experiences which please the senses. Hence you are probably a lover of good food and drink, which may in turn mean you need to keep an eye on the bathroom scales – especially as looking good is also important to you.

Emotionally, you are fairly stable and you stick by your own standards. Taureans do not respond well to change. Intuition also plays an important part in your life.

Moon in Gemini

You have a warm-hearted character, sympathetic and eager to help others. At times reserved, you can also be articulate and chatty: this is part of the paradox of Gemini, which always brings duplicity to its nature. You are interested in current affairs, have a good intellect, are good company and are likely to have many friends. Most of your friends have a high opinion of you and would be ready to defend you should the need arise. However, this is usually unnecessary, as you are quite capable of defending yourself in any verbal confrontation.

Travel is important to your inquisitive mind and you find intellectual stimulus in mixing with people from different cultures. You also gain much from reading, writing and the arts, but you do need plenty of rest and relaxation in order to avoid fatigue.

Moon in Cancer

The Moon in Cancer at the time of birth is a fortunate position as Cancer is the Moon's natural home. This means that the qualities of compassion and understanding given by the Moon are especially enhanced in your nature, and you are friendly, sociable and cope well with emotional pressures. You cherish home and family life, and happily do the domestic tasks. Your surroundings are important to you and you hate squalor and filth. You are likely to have a love of music and poetry.

Your basic character, although at times changeable like the Moon itself, relies on symmetry. You aim to make your surroundings comfortable and harmonious, for yourself and those close to you.

Moon in Leo

The best qualities of the Moon and Leo come together to make you warm-hearted, fair, ambitious and self-confident. With good organisational abilities, you invariably rise to a position of responsibility in your chosen career. This is fortunate as you don't enjoy being an 'also-ran' and would rather be an important part of a small organisation than a menial in a large one.

You should be lucky in love, and happy, provided you put in the effort to make a comfortable home for yourself and those close to you. It is likely that you will have a love of pleasure, sport, music and literature. Life brings you many rewards, most of them as a direct result of your own efforts, although you may be luckier than average and ready to make the best of any situation.

Moon in Virgo

You are endowed with good mental abilities and a keen receptive memory, but you are never ostentatious or pretentious. Naturally quite reserved, you still have many friends, especially of the opposite sex. Marital relationships must be discussed carefully and worked at so that they remain harmonious, as personal attachments can be a problem if you do not give them your full attention.

Talented and persevering, you possess artistic qualities and are a good homemaker. Earning your honours through genuine merit, you work long and hard towards your objectives but show little pride in your achievements. Many short journeys will be undertaken in your life.

Moon in Libra

With the Moon in Libra you are naturally popular and make friends easily. People like you, probably more than you realise. You bring fun to a party and are a natural diplomat. For all its good points, Libra is not the most stable of astrological signs and, as a result, your emotions can be a little unstable too. Therefore, although the Moon in Libra is said to be good for love and marriage, your Sun sign and Rising sign will have an important effect on your emotional and loving qualities.

You must remember to relate to others in your decision-making. Co-operation is crucial because Libra represents the 'balance' of life that can only be achieved through harmonious relationships. Conformity is not easy for you because Libra, an Air sign, defends its independence.

Moon in Scorpio

Some people might call you pushy. In fact, all you really want to do is to live life to the full and protect yourself and your family from the pressures of life. Take care to avoid giving the impression of being sarcastic or impulsive and use your energies wisely and constructively.

You have great courage and you invariably achieve your goals by force of personality and sheer effort. You are fond of mystery and are good at predicting the outcome of situations and events. Travel experiences can be beneficial to you.

You may experience problems if you do not take time to examine your motives in a relationship, and also if you allow jealousy, always a feature of Scorpio, to cloud your judgement.

Moon in Sagittarius

The Moon in Sagittarius helps to make you a generous individual with humanitarian qualities and a kind heart. Restlessness may be intrinsic as your mind is seldom still. Perhaps because of this, you have a need for change that could lead you to several major moves during your adult life. You are not afraid to stand your ground when you know your judgement is right, you speak directly and have good intuition.

At work you are quick, efficient and versatile and so you make an ideal employee. You need work to be intellectually demanding and do not enjoy tedious routines.

In relationships, you anger quickly if faced with stupidity or deception, though you are just as quick to forgive and forget. Emotionally, there are times when your heart rules your head.

Moon in Capricorn

The Moon in Capricorn makes you popular and likely to come into the public eye in some way. The watery Moon is not entirely comfortable in the Earth sign of Capricorn and this may lead to some difficulties in the early years of life. An initial lack of creative ability and indecision must be overcome before the true qualities of patience and perseverance inherent in Capricorn can show through.

You have good administrative ability and are a capable worker, and if you are careful you can accumulate wealth. But you must be cautious and take professional advice in partnerships, as you are open to deception. You may be interested in social or welfare work, which suit your organisational skills and sympathy for others.

Moon in Aquarius

The Moon in Aquarius makes you an active and agreeable person with a friendly, easy-going nature. Sympathetic to the needs of others, you flourish in a laid-back atmosphere. You are broad-minded, fair and open to suggestion, although sometimes you have an unconventional quality which others can find hard to understand.

You are interested in the strange and curious, and in old articles and places. You enjoy trips to these places and gain much from them. Political, scientific and educational work interests you and you might choose a career in science or technology.

Money-wise, you make gains through innovation and concentration and Lunar Aquarians often tackle more than one job at a time. In love you are kind and honest.

Moon in Pisces

You have a kind, sympathetic nature, somewhat retiring at times, but you always take account of others' feelings and help when you can.

Personal relationships may be problematic, but as life goes on you can learn from your experiences and develop a better understanding of yourself and the world around you.

You have a fondness for travel, appreciate beauty and harmony and hate disorder and strife. You may be fond of literature and would make a good writer or speaker yourself. You have a creative imagination and may come across as an incurable romantic. You have strong intuition, maybe bordering on a mediumistic quality, which sets you apart from the mass. You may not be rich in cash terms, but your personal gifts are worth more than gold.

GEMINI IN LOVE

Discover how compatible in love you are with people from the same and other signs of the zodiac. Five stars equals a match made in heaven!

Gemini meets Gemini

Generally speaking, this match can be very successful because although Gemini people can be insecure, they basically feel they are quite 'together' sorts of people. Consequently, they experience a meeting of minds with fellow Twins. This relationship won't work at a distance, and depends on a degree of intimacy to negate the more flighty and showy qualities of the sign. Infidelity could be a potential problem, especially with two Gemini people in the picture, but jealousy doesn't usually prevail. Star rating: ****

Gemini meets Cancer

This is often a very good match. Cancer is a very caring sign and quite adaptable. Geminis are untidy, have butterfly minds and are usually full of a thousand different schemes which Cancerians take in their stride and even relish. They can often be the 'wind beneath the wings' of their Gemini partners. In return, Gemini can eradicate some of the Cancerian emotional insecurity and is more likely to be faithful in thought, word and deed to Cancer than to almost any other sign. Star rating: ****

Gemini meets Leo

There can be problems here, but Gemini is adaptable enough to overcome many of them. Leo is a go-getter and might sometimes rail against Gemini's flighty tendencies, while Gemini's mental disorganisation can undermine Leo's practicality. However, Leo is cheerful and enjoys Gemini's jokey, flippant qualities. At times of personal intimacy, the two signs should be compatible. Leo and Gemini share very high ideals, but Leo will stick at them for longer. Patience is needed on both sides for the relationship to develop. Star rating: ***

Gemini meets Virgo

The fact that both these signs are ruled by the planet Mercury might at first seem good but, unfortunately, Mercury works very differently in each of them. Gemini is untidy, flighty, quick, changeable and easily bored, while Virgo is fastidious, steady and constant. If Virgo is willing to accept some anarchy, all can be well, but this not usually the case. Virgoans are deep thinkers and may find Gemini a little superficial. This pair can be compatible intellectually, though even this side isn't without its problems. Star rating: ***

Gemini meets Libra

One of the best possible zodiac combinations. Libra and Gemini are both Air signs, which leads to a meeting of minds. Both signs simply love to have a good time, although Libra is the tidiest and less forgetful. Gemini's capricious nature won't bother Libra, who acts as a stabilising influence. Life should generally run smoothly, and any rows are likely to be short and sharp. Both parties genuinely like each other, which is of paramount importance in a relationship and, ultimately, there isn't a better reason for being or staying together. Star rating: *****

Gemini meets Scorpio

There could be problems here. Scorpio is one of the deepest and least understood of all the zodiac signs, which at first seems like a challenge to intellectual Gemini, who thinks it can solve anything. But the deeper the Gemini digs, the further down Scorpio goes. Meanwhile, Scorpio may be finding Gemini thoughtless, shallow and even downright annoying. Gemini is often afraid of Scorpio's strength, and the sting in its tail, both of which the perceptive Twins can instinctively recognise. Anything is possible, but the outlook for this match is less than promising. Star rating: **

Gemini meets Sagittarius

A paradoxical relationship this. On paper, the two signs have much in common, but unfortunately, they are often so alike that life turns into a fiercely fought competition. Both signs love change and diversity and both want to be the life and soul of the party. But in life there must always be a leader and a follower, and neither of this pair wants to be second. Both also share a tendency towards infidelity, which may develop into a problem as time passes. This could be an interesting match, but not necessarily successful. Star rating: **

Gemini meets Capricorn

Gemini has a natural fondness for Capricorn, which at first may be mutual. However, Capricorn is very organised, practical and persevering, and always achieves its goals in the end. Gemini starts out like this, but then changes direction on the way, using a more instinctive and evolutionary approach than the Goat that may interfere with the progress of mutual objectives. To compensate, Gemini helps Capricorn to avoid taking itself too seriously, while Capricorn brings a degree of stability into Gemini's world. When this pairing does work, though, it will be spectacular! Star rating: ***

Gemini meets Aquarius

Aquarius is commonly mistaken for a Water sign, but in fact it's ruled by the Air element, and this is the key to its compatibility with Gemini. Both signs mix freely socially, and each has an insatiable curiosity. There is plenty of action, lots of love but very little rest, and so great potential for success if they don't wear each other out! Aquarius revels in its own eccentricity, and encourages Gemini to emulate this. Theirs will be an unconventional household, but almost everyone warms to this crazy and unpredictable couple. Star rating: *****

Gemini meets Pisces

Gemini likes to think of itself as intuitive and intellectual, and indeed sometimes it is, but it will never understand Pisces' dark depths. Another stumbling block is that both Gemini and Pisces are 'split' signs – the Twins and the two Fishes, which means that both are capable of dual personalities. There won't be any shortage of affection, but the real question has to be how much these people ultimately feel they have in common. Pisces is extremely kind, and so is Gemini most of the time. But Pisces does altogether too much soul-searching for Gemini, who might eventually become bored. Star rating: ***

Gemini meets Aries

Don't expect peace and harmony with this combination, although what comes along instead might make up for any disagreements. Gemini has a very fertile imagination, while Aries has the tenacity to make reality from fantasy. Combined, they have a sizzling relationship. There are times when it seems as though both parties will explode with indignation and something has to give. But even if there are clashes, making up will always be most enjoyable! Mutual financial success is very likely in this match. Star rating: ****

Gemini meets Taurus

Gemini people can really infuriate the generally steady Taurean nature as they are so untidy, which is a complete reversal of the Taurean ethos. At first this won't matter; Mr or Miss Gemini is enchanting, entertaining and very different. But time will tell, and that's why this potential relationship only has two stars. There is some hope, however, because Taurus can curb some of the excesses of the Twins, whilst Gemini is more than capable of preventing the Bull from taking itself too seriously. Star rating: **

VENUS:
THE PLANET OF LOVE

If you look up at the sky around sunset or sunrise you will often see Venus in close attendance to the Sun. It is arguably one of the most beautiful sights of all and there is little wonder that historically it became associated with the goddess of love. But although Venus does play an important part in the way you view love and in the way others see you romantically, this is only one of the spheres of influence that it enjoys in your overall character.

Venus has a part to play in the more cultured side of your life and has much to do with your appreciation of art, literature, music and general creativity. Even the way you look is responsive to the part of the zodiac that Venus occupied at the start of your life, though this fact is also down to your Sun sign and Ascending sign. If, at the time you were born, Venus occupied one of the more gregarious zodiac signs, you will be more likely to wear your heart on your sleeve, as well as to be more attracted to entertainment, social gatherings and good company. If on the other hand Venus occupied a quiet zodiac sign at the time of your birth, you would tend to be more retiring and less willing to shine in public situations.

It's good to know what part the planet Venus plays in your life for it can have a great bearing on the way you appear to the rest of the world and since we all have to mix with others, you can learn to make the very best of what Venus has to offer you.

One of the great complications in the past has always been trying to establish exactly what zodiac position Venus enjoyed when you were born because the planet is notoriously difficult to track. However, we have solved that problem by creating a table that is exclusive to your Sun sign, which you will find on the following page.

Establishing your Venus sign could not be easier. Just look up the year of your birth on the following page and you will see a sign of the zodiac. This was the sign that Venus occupied in the period covered by your sign in that year. If Venus occupied more than one sign during the period, this is indicated by the date on which the sign changed, and the name of the new sign. For instance, if you were born in 1950, Venus was in Gemini until the 8th June, after which time it was in Cancer. If you were born before 8th June your Venus sign is Gemini, if you were born on or after 8th June, your Venus sign is Cancer. Once you have established the position of Venus at the time of your birth, you can then look in the pages which follow to see how this has a bearing on your life as a whole.

43

1921 ARIES / 3.6 TAURUS
1922 GEMINI / 26.5 CANCER /
    21.6 LEO
1923 TAURUS / 15.6 GEMINI
1924 CANCER
1925 GEMINI / 9.6 CANCER
1926 ARIES / 2.6 TAURUS
1927 CANCER / 8.6 LEO
1928 TAURUS / 30.5 GEMINI
1929 ARIES / 4.6 TAURUS
1930 GEMINI / 22.5 CANCER /
    21.6 LEO
1931 TAURUS / 15.6 GEMINI
1932 CANCER
1933 GEMINI / 9.6 CANCER
1934 ARIES / 2.6 TAURUS
1935 CANCER / 8.6 LEO
1936 TAURUS / 30.5 GEMINI
1937 ARIES / 4.6 TAURUS
1938 GEMINI / 25.5 CANCER /
    20.6 LEO
1939 TAURUS / 14.6 GEMINI
1940 CANCER
1941 CANCER / 7.6 LEO
1942 GEMINI / 8.6 CANCER
1943 ARIES / 1.6 TAURUS
1944 CANCER / 7.6 LEO
1945 TAURUS / 29.5 GEMINI
1946 ARIES / 5.6 TAURUS
1947 GEMINI / 24.5 CANCER /
    19.6 LEO
1948 TAURUS / 14.6 GEMINI
1949 CANCER
1950 GEMINI / 8.6 CANCER
1951 ARIES / 1.6 TAURUS
1952 TAURUS / 29.5 GEMINI
1953 ARIES / 5.6 TAURUS
1954 GEMINI / 24.5 CANCER /
    19.6 LEO
1955 TAURUS / 13.6 GEMINI
1956 CANCER
1957 GEMINI / 7.6 CANCER
1958 ARIES / 31.5 TAURUS
1959 CANCER / 7.6 LEO
1960 TAURUS / 28.5 GEMINI
1961 ARIES / 6.6 TAURUS
1962 GEMINI / 24.5 CANCER /
    18.6 LEO
1963 TAURUS / 13.6 GEMINI
1964 CANCER / 17.6 GEMINI
1965 GEMINI / 7.6 CANCER
1966 ARIES / 31.5 TAURUS
1967 CANCER / 7.6 LEO
1968 TAURUS / 28.5 GEMINI
1969 ARIES / 6.6 TAURUS
1970 GEMINI / 23.5 CANCER /
    18.5 LEO
1971 TAURUS / 12.6 GEMINI
1972 CANCER / 12.6 GEMINI

1973 GEMINI / 6.6 CANCER
1974 ARIES / 30.5 TAURUS
1975 CANCER / 7.6 LEO
1976 TAURUS / 27.5 GEMINI
1977 ARIES / 7.6 TAURUS
1978 GEMINI / 23.5 CANCER /
    17.5 LEO
1979 TAURUS / 12.6 GEMINI
1980 CANCER / 6.6 GEMINI
1981 GEMINI / 6.6 CANCER
1982 ARIES / 30.5 TAURUS
1983 CANCER / 6.6 LEO
1984 TAURUS / 27.5 GEMINI /
    21.6 CANCER
1985 ARIES / 7.6 TAURUS
1986 GEMINI / 22.5 CANCER /
    17.5 LEO
1987 TAURUS / 11.6 GEMINI
1988 CANCER / 27.5 GEMINI
1989 GEMINI / 5.6 CANCER
1990 ARIES / 29.5 TAURUS
1991 CANCER / 6.6 LEO
1992 TAURUS / 26.5 GEMINI /
    20.6 LEO
1993 ARIES / 7.6 TAURUS
1994 CANCER / 16.6 LEO
1995 TAURUS / 11.6 GEMINI
1996 CANCER / 27.5 GEMINI
1997 GEMINI / 4.6 CANCER
1998 ARIES / 29.5 TAURUS
1999 CANCER / 6.6 LEO
2000 TAURUS / 25.5 GEMINI /
    19.6 CANCER
2001 ARIES / 7.6 TAURUS
2002 CANCER / 15.6 LEO
2003 TAURUS / 11.6 GEMINI
2004 CANCER / 27.5 GEMINI
2005 GEMINI / 2.6 CANCER
2006 ARIES / 29.6 TAURUS
2007 CANCER / 6.6 LEO
2008 TAURUS / 25.5 GEMINI /
    19.6 CANCER
2009 ARIES / 7.6 TAURUS
2010 CANCER / 15.6 LEO
2011 TAURUS / 11.6 GEMINI
2012 CANCER / 27.5 GEMINI
2013 GEMINI / 2.6 CANCER
2014 ARIES / 29.6 TAURUS
2015 CANCER / 6.6 LEO
2016 GEMINI / 18.6 CANCER
2017 GEMINI / 7.6 CANCER
2018 CANCER / 15.6 LEO
2019 TAURUS / 11.6 GEMINI

VENUS THROUGH THE ZODIAC SIGNS

Venus in Aries

Amongst other things, the position of Venus in Aries indicates a fondness for travel, music and all creative pursuits. Your nature tends to be affectionate and you would try not to create confusion or difficulty for others if it could be avoided. Many people with this planetary position have a great love of the theatre, and mental stimulation is of the greatest importance. Early romantic attachments are common with Venus in Aries, so it is very important to establish a genuine sense of romantic continuity. Early marriage is not recommended, especially if it is based on sympathy. You may give your heart a little too readily on occasions.

Venus in Taurus

You are capable of very deep feelings and your emotions tend to last for a very long time. This makes you a trusting partner and lover, whose constancy is second to none. In life you are precise and careful and always try to do things the right way. Although this means an ordered life, which you are comfortable with, it can also lead you to be rather too fussy for your own good. Despite your pleasant nature, you are very fixed in your opinions and quite able to speak your mind. Others are attracted to you and historical astrologers always quoted this position of Venus as being very fortunate in terms of marriage. However, if you find yourself involved in a failed relationship, it could take you a long time to trust again.

Venus in Gemini

As with all associations related to Gemini, you tend to be quite versatile, anxious for change and intelligent in your dealings with the world at large. You may gain money from more than one source but you are equally good at spending it. There is an inference here that you are a good communicator, via either the written or the spoken word, and you love to be in the company of interesting people. Always on the look-out for culture, you may also be very fond of music, and love to indulge the curious and cultured side of your nature. In romance you tend to have more than one relationship and could find yourself associated with someone who has previously been a friend or even a distant relative.

Venus in Cancer

You often stay close to home because you are very fond of family and enjoy many of your most treasured moments when you are with those you love. Being naturally sympathetic, you will always do anything you can to support those around you, even people you hardly know at all. This charitable side of your nature is your most noticeable trait and is one of the reasons why others are naturally so fond of you. Being receptive and in some cases even psychic, you can see through to the soul of most of those with whom you come into contact. You may not commence too many romantic attachments but when you do give your heart, it tends to be unconditionally.

Venus in Leo

It becomes quickly obvious to almost anyone you meet that you are kind, sympathetic and yet determined enough to stand up for anyone or anything that is truly important to you. Bright and sunny, you warm the world with your natural enthusiasm and would rarely do anything to hurt those around you, or at least not intentionally. In romance you are ardent and sincere, though some may find your style just a little overpowering. Gains come through your contacts with other people and this could be especially true with regard to romance, for love and money often come hand in hand for those who were born with Venus in Leo. People claim to understand you, though you are more complex than you seem.

Venus in Virgo

Your nature can be fairly quiet no matter what your Sun sign, though this fact often manifests itself as inner peace and would not prevent you from being sociable. Some delays, and even the odd disappointment, in love cannot be ruled out with this planetary position, though it's a fact that you will usually find the happiness you look for in the end. Catapulting yourself into romantic entanglements that you know to be rather ill-advised is not sensible, and it would be better to wait before you commit yourself exclusively to any one person. It is the essence of your nature to serve the world at large and through doing so it is possible that you will attract money at some stage in your life.

Venus in Libra

Venus is very comfortable in Libra and bestows upon those people who have this planetary position a particular sort of kindness that is easy to recognise. This is a very good position for all sorts of friendships and also for romantic attachments that usually bring much joy into your life. Few individuals with Venus in Libra would avoid marriage and since you are capable of great depths of love, it is likely that you will find a contented personal life. You like to mix with people of integrity and intelligence, but don't take kindly to scruffy surroundings or any work where you get your hands too dirty. Careful speculation, good business dealings and money through marriage all seem fairly likely.

Venus in Scorpio

You are quite open and tend to spend money quite freely, even on those occasions when you don't have very much. Although your intentions are always good, there are times when you get yourself into the odd scrape and this can be particularly true when it comes to romance, which you may come to late or from a rather unexpected direction. Certainly you have the power to be happy and to make others contented on the way, but you find the odd stumbling block on your journey through life and it could seem that you have to work harder than those around you. As a result of this, you gain a much deeper understanding of the true value of personal happiness than many people ever do, and are likely to achieve true contentment in the end.

Venus in Sagittarius

You are lighthearted, cheerful and always able to see the funny side of any situation. These facts enhance your popularity, which is especially high with members of the opposite sex. You should never have to look too far to find romantic interest in your life, though it is just possible that you might be too willing to commit yourself before you are certain that the person in question is right for you. Part of the problem here extends to other areas of life too. The fact is that you like variety in everything and so can tire of situations that fail to offer it. All the same, if you choose wisely and learn to understand your restless side, then great happiness can be yours.

Venus in Capricorn

The most notable trait that comes from Venus in this position is that it makes you trustworthy and able to take on all sorts of responsibilities in life. People are instinctively fond of you and love you all the more because you are always ready to help those who are in any form of need. Social and business popularity can be yours and there is a magnetic quality to your nature that is particularly attractive in a romantic sense. Anyone who wants a partner for a lover, a spouse and a good friend too would almost certainly look in your direction. Constancy is the hallmark of your nature and unfaithfulness would go right against the grain. You might sometimes be a little too trusting.

Venus in Aquarius

This location of Venus offers a fondness for travel and a desire to try out something new at every possible opportunity. You are extremely easy to get along with and tend to have many friends from varied backgrounds, classes and inclinations. You like to live a distinct sort of life and gain a great deal from moving about, both in a career sense and with regard to your home. It is not out of the question that you could form a romantic attachment to someone who comes from far away or be attracted to a person of a distinctly artistic and original nature. What you cannot stand is jealousy, for you have friends of both sexes and would want to keep things that way.

Venus in Pisces

The first thing people tend to notice about you is your wonderful, warm smile. Being very charitable by nature you will do anything to help others, even if you don't know them well. Much of your life may be spent sorting out situations for other people, but it is very important to feel that you are living for yourself too. In the main, you remain cheerful and tend to be quite attractive to members of the opposite sex. Where romantic attachments are concerned, you could be drawn to people who are significantly older or younger than yourself, or to someone with a unique career or point of view. It might be best for you to avoid marrying whilst you are still very young.

GEMINI:
2018 DIARY PAGES

October
2018

1 MONDAY
Moon Age Day 22   Moon Sign Gemini

It's time to focus on what is really important to you, especially in practical terms. You have what it takes to get ahead and to stay there, even if one or two people seem to be doing what they can to prevent you from moving on. The lunar high gives you extra energy, more ingenuity and it also steps up your sense of humour no end.

2 TUESDAY
Moon Age Day 23   Moon Sign Cancer

Certain professional pressures could be slightly hard to handle and if this is the case you will need to be quite circumspect in your handling of colleagues. Personal issues are less contentious or difficult and you might be turning heads when you are appearing in any public setting. You should also be very creative under present trends.

3 WEDNESDAY
Moon Age Day 24   Moon Sign Cancer

Focus today on the better side of people's nature and do what you can to encourage those around you to be kind to each other. If this makes you seem like some sort of saint, you can at least rest easy in the fact that you will be employing the odd dubious technique in order to get what you want in a financial sense!

4 THURSDAY
Moon Age Day 25   Moon Sign Leo

Social and teamwork events are now highlighted, even if you sometimes feel that you are not quite on the same wavelength as those with whom you are co-operating. Stand by your past judgements, especially in home-based matters, but be aware that a degree of flexibility also necessary.

5 FRIDAY
Moon Age Day 26   Moon Sign Leo

Romantically, today could be a bit of a downer. Issues associated with affairs of the heart probably need more thinking about and you may not strike the right chord when it comes to impressing someone you care for a lot. This is all very temporary and it won't be long before you are singing love's sweet song again.

6 SATURDAY
Moon Age Day 27   Moon Sign Virgo

Your main area of satisfaction today seems to come from anything to do with communication. You are very explicit in both your desires and requests around now and will leave nobody in any doubt as to what you want. Take definite action and you will avoid mistakes and reach your objectives that much quicker.

7 SUNDAY
Moon Age Day 28   Moon Sign Virgo

Family and domestic situations are now likely to be good. Your home life will seem slightly more comfortable and you should be able to get on side with those who haven't seemed to listen to you all that much lately. There should be a good feeling of harmony around and that allows you to move certain plans forward successfully.

8 MONDAY
Moon Age Day 29   Moon Sign Virgo

You tend to be very searching in your conversations at this time and you will be anxious to know exactly what other people mean. Although this can be a little tedious on occasions it does at least leave you in no doubt as to what you are up against. Gemini really does need to work on certainties now, not questions.

9 TUESDAY
Moon Age Day 0   Moon Sign Libra

Circumstances may seem to conspire to limit your effectiveness, especially in a working environment. Your sense of originality and independence are both somewhat restricted and you might find yourself having to do certain things because of the expectations of others. At home you will be freer to do what suits you best.

10 WEDNESDAY   *Moon Age Day 1   Moon Sign Libra*

Although certain aspects of life might seem to be something of a chore as the midweek period arrives, there are ways and means of enjoying even the most tedious jobs. The more you share things with your partner and family members, the better you will be the prospects for laughter; and you do need to smile a lot at the moment.

11 THURSDAY   *Moon Age Day 2   Moon Sign Scorpio*

Although some circumstances may seem to work against you today, that's not the way things are likely to turn out in the end. True, you might have to take a rather strange route to some of the destinations that are on your mind, but you will get there in the end. On the way you can achieve a great deal in terms of self-appreciation.

12 FRIDAY   *Moon Age Day 3   Moon Sign Scorpio*

You can be of great help to other people today, sometimes without even realising that you have done anything at all. You are often an inspiration, partly because you are generally so cheerful and because you don't give in when things get slightly tough. You will also be showing the more courageous side of your nature around this time.

13 SATURDAY   *Moon Age Day 4   Moon Sign Sagittarius*

The lunar low might dampen your spirits, though if you settle for a steady day and don't expect too much you may hardly notice that anything is different. You might come unstuck if you decide to pit yourself against the world, so don't try that. It would be like knocking your head against a wall.

14 SUNDAY   *Moon Age Day 5   Moon Sign Sagittarius*

Bear in mind that the most important thing today is to be as much use to others as you can manage. Look around in your work environment for things you can do to lighten the load of your comrades, but wherever possible stick to tasks you understand very well. You won't get far if you try to be a trailblazer, at least not until tomorrow at least.

15 MONDAY   *Moon Age Day 6   Moon Sign Capricorn*

Now you can make the most from social groups and as long as the affection you are dealing in is fairly superficial, you can't go wrong. Teamwork should go well and you seem to have what it takes to be in charge without anyone realising. As a result what happens is actually down to you, but everyone thinks they are a winner.

16 TUESDAY   *Moon Age Day 7   Moon Sign Capricorn*

Check and double-check everything. On a practical level, you cannot afford to take anything for granted today. This is especially true where travel plans are concerned. If you feel restless at the moment, it is important to ring the changes. A total change of scene would do you good, preferably in the company of your partner.

17 WEDNESDAY   *Moon Age Day 8   Moon Sign Capricorn*

It looks as though for today at least you will relish the chance to meet people who you might consider to be either famous, or at least worthy of your adoration. You may also enjoy a little notoriety yourself right now, and certainly will not shy away from the chance to shine in any social setting. Money matters are variable at present.

18 THURSDAY   *Moon Age Day 9   Moon Sign Aquarius*

Avoid too many hasty or impulsive actions today. You don't need to shy away from making decisions, but simply take time to think first. Trends suggest that people from the past could be finding their way to your door and they could bring happy memories with them.

19 FRIDAY   *Moon Age Day 10   Moon Sign Aquarius*

Socially and romantically your powers of attraction are increasing rapidly. Good judgement proves to be very important so be discriminating in your approach to all professional and practical matters. Look out for a slight increase in your fortune as time advances, brought about partly through ingenuity.

20 SATURDAY
Moon Age Day 11   Moon Sign Pisces

Don't believe everything you hear from others today. It is possible to be too trusting and if you are, there is a chance you will come quite badly unstuck further down the road. Take everything with a pinch of salt and think most things through for yourself. Even usually reliable sources are suspect now.

21 SUNDAY
Moon Age Day 12   Moon Sign Pisces

Your opinionated nature might get you into hot water today – that is unless you put the brakes on a little and think carefully before you speak. Outbursts of any sort are to be studiously avoided and you would do well today to count to ten on a number of occasions. Most things can be put right later, but one or two could be difficult.

22 MONDAY
Moon Age Day 13   Moon Sign Pisces

Your focus is now on work and in particular on the assistance you are able to offer to other people. Acknowledging the contribution made by colleagues is only fair, and at the same time it helps to increase your own personal popularity. There is something quite impulsive about the way you deal with domestic and family issues today.

23 TUESDAY
Moon Age Day 14   Moon Sign Aries

The relaxed and sociable mood you demonstrate to the world during the second half of today is likely to be very infectious. People generally warm to your positive nature and sociable disposition. Since popularity is quite important to Gemini, you should be very pleased with the attention you are getting from those around you.

24 WEDNESDAY
Moon Age Day 15   Moon Sign Aries

What a great time this would be for some wheeling and dealing. If you have something to sell, this could be the best time to find a buyer and you might be especially good when dealing on internet sites. In most respects, you are ingenious and you know what you are looking for.

25 THURSDAY

Moon Age Day 16   Moon Sign Taurus

Things seem to be going better in the social world right now than they have since before last weekend. If you have been subject to delays or difficulties of one sort or another, these should now disappear and you seem to be quicker to respond to specific situations. Money matters are likely to be less troublesome too.

26 FRIDAY

Moon Age Day 17   Moon Sign Taurus

This might be one of the best days of the month to spend some time alone. For today the Moon is passing through your solar twelfth house, which is certain to make you more pensive and inclined to retreat somewhat from the hurly-burly of everyday life. Like everyone else, your mind needs meditation.

27 SATURDAY

Moon Age Day 18   Moon Sign Gemini

Be ready to back your innovative ideas, which are coming thick and fast while the lunar high is around. Make the most of all social and business contacts and take comfort from the fact that people seem to be queuing up to be your friend. In addition you should find that your luck has increased.

28 SUNDAY

Moon Age Day 19   Moon Sign Gemini

Confidence and enthusiasm are your keywords for today. Although you might be limited as to how much you can do in a business sense on a Sunday, you can still make up a great deal of ground just by thinking in the right way. You are especially innovative at the moment and will be proving it all day long.

29 MONDAY

Moon Age Day 20   Moon Sign Cancer

It looks as though powerful emotions are stirred at home and it's difficult to get your message across in quite the way you might wish. Trends are improving though. They bring you greater determination and help you to find the right words. In friendships you should now find yourself extremely popular.

30 TUESDAY   *Moon Age Day 21   Moon Sign Cancer*

Events might be slightly confusing today and for a zodiac sign that is always on the ball this can seem to be something of a problem. The best way out of such situations is to smile at yourself and carry on regardless. Anything that does trouble you is likely to be out of the way before many too hours have passed.

31 WEDNESDAY   *Moon Age Day 22   Moon Sign Cancer*

You are charming and magnetic in terms of the way you approach those around you, particularly members of the opposite sex. Social activities should continue to go well and you can find ways of getting ahead by saying and doing the right things. The approach of winter is on your mind and might spell changes at home.

♊ November 2018

1 THURSDAY
Moon Age Day 23   Moon Sign Leo

You may not have as many opportunities as often seems to be the case but even a single option is worth following and can lead to the gains you always want from life. Instead of diversifying as much as you would normally do, try to focus on specifics. Your partner should now be very supportive.

2 FRIDAY
Moon Age Day 24   Moon Sign Leo

Some slight dissatisfaction with certain relationships could now have you looking at people you don't know very well and wondering if they could become trusted friends. Make sure that you understand what is really going on before you suspect an existing pal of being disloyal and try to avoid being over judgemental right now.

3 SATURDAY
Moon Age Day 25   Moon Sign Virgo

Be sure that you have a clear understanding of what other people mean before you allow yourself to become involved in their schemes. In reality this is not a good time to get yourself too enmeshed in anything that looks even slightly suspect because you are a tad more gullible than would normally be the case. Ask a friend for advice.

4 SUNDAY
Moon Age Day 26   Moon Sign Virgo

This would be a good day during which to step back and look again at some of your initiatives in the professional and practical world. It is possible that you are missing out on something so simple you are looking right over the top of it. Don't carry burdens around that you can easily offload.

5 MONDAY   *Moon Age Day 27   Moon Sign Libra*

Your personal objectives and ideas for the future tend to be inspired and new discussions with others can prove to be helpful as you begin to put things into place. Plan now to travel later, but also make short excursions if you possibly can. Time spent with family members today is likely to be comfortable and satisfying.

6 TUESDAY   *Moon Age Day 28   Moon Sign Libra*

Your powers are not at their strongest and you may need to call for support over something you don't fully understand. There are vital issues to sort out as far as your personal life is concerned, but there are experts around who can be of assistance to you so there is no need to go it alone – except for the sake of misguided pride.

7 WEDNESDAY   *Moon Age Day 0   Moon Sign Scorpio*

Communications are positively highlighted so this is a time that is very conducive when it comes to researching and gaining the information you need to get ahead in the days and weeks to come. Any sort of plan for the future will require modification and the sort of tinkering you don't usually have time to consider. Spend a few moments doing so now.

8 THURSDAY   *Moon Age Day 1   Moon Sign Scorpio*

In some respects you are out there on your own, which is where you enjoy being. Although Gemini is a great team player, you are born under an Air sign and that means you are basically a solo-performer in terms of achieving personal success. It is the conjoining of these two elements of your nature that makes you powerful.

9 FRIDAY   *Moon Age Day 2   Moon Sign Sagittarius*

Circumstances still seem to block you at every turn and making the sort of headway you would wish won't be easy until Sunday at least. For now you should stand and wait. That isn't easy for Gemini but it does mean you will keep your powder dry and that you will be in the right position to get on well later.

10 SATURDAY   *Moon Age Day 3   Moon Sign Sagittarius*

Gradually you will see how well things are turning out for you – at least you will if you manage to stay fairly quiet and contemplative during today. Without any effort on your part you should be making a really good impression when it counts the most and you can rely on the good offices of colleagues and friends.

11 SUNDAY   *Moon Age Day 4   Moon Sign Sagittarius*

There might be a few ups and downs as far as money is concerned, but when it comes to the sort of success that cannot be counted in financial terms you are likely to do very well indeed. What you have is greater prestige and a more concrete knowledge of what you have to do to influence and impress the most important people.

12 MONDAY   *Moon Age Day 5   Moon Sign Capricorn*

All aspects of communication come under the spotlight today and you will not be found lacking when it comes to getting your message across in a very positive and stimulating way. There is much to be done but you won't really help yourself by trying to do it all at the same time. Be ordered in your day and also careful.

13 TUESDAY   *Moon Age Day 6   Moon Sign Capricorn*

You will enjoy almost anything that is happening around you, especially if you are the one who arranged it. Last-minute details are dealt with in a moment and you will not allow any sort of delay to get in the way of your search for adventure. Nobody is likely to be more inspirational than you right now.

14 WEDNESDAY   *Moon Age Day 7   Moon Sign Aquarius*

Your desire to be of service to others can mean you are taken advantage off on some occasions, which is something to watch out for. It doesn't really matter though because you have plenty to give and there is no end to your present generosity. Not everyone will love you, but when it matters the most you gain respect.

15 THURSDAY   *Moon Age Day 8   Moon Sign Aquarius*

You are now likely to be extremely susceptible to the influence of other people. This is not too surprising because you never like to be isolated and you are bound to fall under the sway of charismatic types. However, the influence is even stronger now and you could be inclined to look up to someone rather too much for your own good, so be aware.

16 FRIDAY   *Moon Age Day 9   Moon Sign Aquarius*

This is a time when you should definitely not hide your light under a bushel. You need to let everyone know what you are capable of achieving and that way you will start to believe it yourself. There are some real coups possible for you now and you may get plenty of support from other Geminis.

17 SATURDAY   ☿   *Moon Age Day 10   Moon Sign Pisces*

You ought to be having some rewarding and enjoyable moments today, especially where your love life is concerned but also on the social scene. If you can't manage to promote quite the same dynamic profile you usually do, you can take comfort in the fact that many people love you for what you truly are.

18 SUNDAY   ☿   *Moon Age Day 11   Moon Sign Pisces*

You are going to be very sensitive to atmosphere today – in some ways probably too much. On the positive side you are clearly very charitable and giving during this interlude and almost anyone could approach you for help. In truth, you are probably better at helping those around you today than you are at assisting yourself.

19 MONDAY   ☿   *Moon Age Day 12   Moon Sign Aries*

Try to assert yourself positively and confidently at work today as new ventures are likely to work out well and you can display a generally confident face to the world. Co-workers are likely to be more co-operative than might have been the case for the last week or more and you are clearly in the market for little adventures.

20 TUESDAY ☿ *Moon Age Day 13   Moon Sign Aries*

Generally, you can now do worse than to follow your instincts, which should not lead you astray. There will be occasions when sound common sense isn't all that useful because some situations won't be following a logical path. Being able to cope with the twists and turns of life is what sets Gemini apart.

21 WEDNESDAY ☿ *Moon Age Day 14   Moon Sign Taurus*

Now there are likely to be more good things happening socially, which together with an improved personal scene should see you getting more optimistic by the day. Rules and regulations won't impress you in the slightest, even if you have to follow some of them for the moment. Many Geminis are now actively planning a long and exciting journey.

22 THURSDAY ☿ *Moon Age Day 15   Moon Sign Taurus*

It looks as though you need to go your own way when it comes to your career, even if that means going against the wishes of someone close to you. This shouldn't be a problem because you have it within yourself right now to be very diplomatic and you won't willingly upset anyone when a few well-chosen words can avoid it.

23 FRIDAY ☿ *Moon Age Day 16   Moon Sign Taurus*

You could be prone to sudden periods of withdrawal from worldly affairs and your intuition will be stimulated significantly by meditation. If you spend some time looking inside yourself, you might find things there that will surprise you. What Gemini appears to be on the surface is very different to what lies beneath.

24 SATURDAY ☿ *Moon Age Day 17   Moon Sign Gemini*

The time is now right to capitalise on all your efforts during the last few weeks. Things should be starting to mature and you are in the right frame of mind to move ahead progressively on a number of different fronts. Energy and good fortune are both with you, and those you rely on assist you.

25 SUNDAY ☿ *Moon Age Day 18   Moon Sign Gemini*

This may be one of the best days of the month for making fresh starts and initiating new ideas. Just about anything you do at present seems to be tinged with an element of good fortune and you will also be quite inventive and inspirational. People from the past are inclined to re-emerge into your life at any time in the days ahead.

26 MONDAY ☿ *Moon Age Day 19   Moon Sign Cancer*

You may find that some emotions, particularly at home, are very close to the surface at present. This means that you could be rather touchier than would normally be the case. Try to find ways today to enjoy yourself and put some responsibilities on the back burner. Family members should do their best to be accommodating.

27 TUESDAY ☿ *Moon Age Day 20   Moon Sign Cancer*

It seems likely that personal and domestic matters will have an element of the irrational about them just now, though this is hardly likely to be coming from your direction. Your usual boisterous energies are stepped up no end as the day wears on, pointing you in the direction of a much more progressive phase ahead.

28 WEDNESDAY ☿ *Moon Age Day 21   Moon Sign Leo*

If there is a battle of wills around today, it wouldn't be surprising to discover that you are getting involved, which really isn't all that useful. Allow the easy-going qualities of Gemini to predominate and avoid reactions that others would see as threatening. On the whole you should be feeling good about yourself today.

29 THURSDAY ☿ *Moon Age Day 22   Moon Sign Leo*

It is important to encourage a sense of change and variety in your life. Try to set out on a journey that leads to new intellectual experiences. Travel is positively highlighted right now and would certainly stimulate those little grey cells. The advice you offer others at this stage tends to be rational and wise.

30 FRIDAY ☿ *Moon Age Day 23 Moon Sign Virgo*

A professional matter may fail to turn up trumps for you today and you might need to enlist the support of some elusive people. As a result there might be a few attendant frustrations to be dealt with, but you should get through these relatively easily. Don't expect today to be plain sailing, but it should be quite interesting.

II

December 2018

1 SATURDAY ☿ *Moon Age Day 24 Moon Sign Virgo*

You may now be quite impulsive when it comes to the acquisition of material things, especially when it comes to Christmas presents. Save your money for a few more days because better bargains could be on the way. It might only now have occurred to you to check your diary carefully for this weekend.

2 SUNDAY ☿ *Moon Age Day 25 Moon Sign Libra*

Domestic matters seem to be favoured during this part of the weekend. It is possible that you are turning your attention to festive matters – for example have you purchased your tree or taken the decorations from the attic? These are jobs that have to be done but for the moment you are more concerned with enjoying yourself.

3 MONDAY ☿ *Moon Age Day 26 Moon Sign Libra*

Impatience with practical things is part of the astrological picture at this time. You won't be all that happy with any sort of machine or electrical gadget that seems determined to cross you, though your patience with people is about to become legendary. Fortunately you will only be kicking gadgets!

4 TUESDAY ☿ *Moon Age Day 27 Moon Sign Scorpio*

Existing attachments will probably be slightly less important to you at the moment than ones that have recently begun. Try not to push your old friends out of the way because you will need them again eventually. Someone you haven't seen for a long time could be coming back into your life in a big way.

5 WEDNESDAY ☿ *Moon Age Day 28 Moon Sign Scorpio*

Avoid making spur-of-the-moment decisions, especially when it comes to your love life. Make sure that you have checked everything you intend to do with those around you and explain yourself more than once if you sense this is necessary. Don't be too quick to take offence with a friend when it is obvious that none was intended.

6 THURSDAY ☿ *Moon Age Day 29 Moon Sign Scorpio*

Despite a sense of vigour and determination there are obstacles to get over today that you might not find easy to negotiate. It looks as though the way forward is to trust others, though this isn't always easy for some Geminis who prefer to be out there at the front. Experts are experts though, and you can't know everything yourself.

7 FRIDAY *Moon Age Day 0 Moon Sign Sagittarius*

You could easily benefit from a quiet day today because before the day is over you will be subject to the lunar low. This is unlikely to have too much of a bearing on your life whilst the Sun remains in its present position but you may decide that the time is right for a well-earned rest and for some pampering.

8 SATURDAY *Moon Age Day 1 Moon Sign Sagittarius*

You could still be in rest mode and won't be all that keen to take on anything totally new or particularly difficult. This isn't like you and you might kick yourself for being something of a wimp. Actually this is merely a regeneration phase and nothing at all is lost from taking your time or from deciding that discretion is the better part of valour.

9 SUNDAY *Moon Age Day 2 Moon Sign Capricorn*

Upsets in personal relationships seem to be par for the course as December progresses. Don't take these too seriously and learn to laugh at yourself for being precious or difficult. If you do this, you won't have much trouble remaining popular with friends.

10 MONDAY   *Moon Age Day 3   Moon Sign Capricorn*

Your romantic life could throw up some challenges, but none of these are likely to prove difficult for you to deal with. On the contrary you have real panache and will be good at turning heads in almost any situation. Whether you know exactly what to say when you have some amazing person's attention remains to be seen.

11 TUESDAY   *Moon Age Day 4   Moon Sign Aquarius*

Romance and personal attachments are boosted enormously around now. In terms of your social life you will have little or no difficulty getting on the right side of the most important people and you are more than aware who can be of help to you. Despite this it is clear that in every important way you give just as much as you get.

12 WEDNESDAY   *Moon Age Day 5   Moon Sign Aquarius*

You should enjoy the chance to work hard at this time, partly because you know that you will benefit almost directly from the effort you are now putting in. Once you get started on any project you will be quick and efficient in the way you deal with it. This should be a period of quite satisfactory results and new plans for the future.

13 THURSDAY   *Moon Age Day 6   Moon Sign Aquarius*

The influences today should offer you more time for leisure and romance. Don't spend too much time today on pointless or tedious chores. Your social life should certainly be on a winning streak and being the sort of person you are, you are probably in a Christmas frame of mind already.

14 FRIDAY   *Moon Age Day 7   Moon Sign Pisces*

The ability to work hard, coupled with determined ambition can get you a long way now. There are excellent professional possibilities about and your achievements can be quite significant. On the negative side, you may be slightly short tempered and inclined to snap somewhat if people make mistakes.

15 SATURDAY
Moon Age Day 8   Moon Sign Pisces

At times some of your objectives can be slightly confusing and that is probably because you are trying to do too much, all at the same time. In one particular area you could be within sight of the winning post but the effort you put in as you get there may need to be that much greater. Always keep your promises.

16 SUNDAY
Moon Age Day 9   Moon Sign Pisces

A lack of emotional objectivity could cause you to be tetchy and you won't have the level of patience with loved ones that would usually be the case. Rather than falling out with anyone, keep yourself to yourself, although this might cause those around you to wonder what is wrong and to keep asking you.

17 MONDAY
Moon Age Day 10   Moon Sign Aries

A period of intense feelings and emotional conflicts is possible. You need to make some significant changes but you may not be entirely sure what these will be. As a result you could spend the day on tenterhooks and feel ill at ease with yourself. Rely on your good communication skills and keep talking to anyone who will listen.

18 TUESDAY
Moon Age Day 11   Moon Sign Aries

Attracting the benefits of life should not be very difficult and that means more money and greater luxuries. These things are fine, just as long as you don't allow them to be in charge of you – and there is always this danger for Gemini. The really important things in your life cost nothing and you won't tire of them.

19 WEDNESDAY
Moon Age Day 12   Moon Sign Taurus

Today there could be minor complications at home, but probably not for long or in any serious way. You have your sights set on the festive season and you are probably stepping up your social life already. If you haven't got the decorations out yet, this might be a happy and nostalgic way to spend part of today.

20 THURSDAY   *Moon Age Day 13   Moon Sign Taurus*

Socially speaking you encounter plenty of light-hearted moments. Of course this is to be expected because Christmas is just around the corner. Unfortunately, you won't find everyone around you quite as jolly and carefree as you might be. Dealing with grumpy types is something you may have to get used to at this time.

21 FRIDAY   *Moon Age Day 14   Moon Sign Gemini*

You might have to put up with feeling second-best in some relationships, probably because others have their own lives to lead and cannot be paying you all their attention. This doesn't suit you at all at this time and you could be rather too demanding for your own good. Try a little humility and some empathy.

22 SATURDAY   *Moon Age Day 15   Moon Sign Gemini*

This ought to be a good period for letting your hair down and for making the best possible impression on the world around you. The lunar high makes you energetic and also inclines you to put yourself in the driving seat. You should be so confident at this stage that it won't occur to others to question your motives or style.

23 SUNDAY   *Moon Age Day 16   Moon Sign Cancer*

There are plenty of good ideas around today, but whether or not you will have sufficient energy or determination to see them through to completion remains to be seen. Keep your aspirations within reasonable reach and don't expect too much of yourself. Be willing to accept some help.

24 MONDAY   *Moon Age Day 17   Moon Sign Cancer*

Christmas Eve is likely to bring a very sentimental attitude on your part and almost everything you do is likely to be geared towards your family. Wherever it proves to be possible you will want to spend time at home, though there is also an urge to travel – a dichotomy that might confuse you. Look up an old friend when evening comes.

25 TUESDAY
Moon Age Day 18   Moon Sign Leo

With your mind and body so active under the influence of Mercury, you can be a real live wire and you will be quite happy to get involved in anything that is going on in your vicinity. Energy levels are especially high and you are quite physically motivated, as well as having a lightning-quick mind.

26 WEDNESDAY
Moon Age Day 19   Moon Sign Leo

The day after Christmas could find you somewhat pensive, but determined to solve some puzzles that presently have a bearing on your life. Get to grips with situations that have been waiting for a while as now you have the time to address them. Sitting and doing nothing certainly isn't going to be an option for you at this time.

27 THURSDAY
Moon Age Day 20   Moon Sign Virgo

You might be quite emotionally motivated today and will be showing your very human side to the world at large. Beware of reacting too strongly to specific events, particularly at times when you know that a steady attitude is more impressive. You might have to bite your tongue in discussions with superiors.

28 FRIDAY
Moon Age Day 21   Moon Sign Virgo

It looks as though you will insist on being the centre of attention today, which is probably no bad thing. On the way you brighten the lives of people who might have been rather down in the dumps of late. Family members and friends alike benefit from your present state of mind and show you as much kindness as you are delivering.

29 SATURDAY
Moon Age Day 22   Moon Sign Libra

Professionally speaking, you work best when you can follow your own dictates and when others don't have control over your time or resources. This might mean letting someone know politely that you intend to go it alone. Outside of practical matters the social scene begins to get busier and there won't be much time to spare.

30 SUNDAY   *Moon Age Day 23   Moon Sign Libra*

Whatever you do today, it needs to have meaning and purpose. Don't waste hours on trivial matters and be sure that when you start something new, it is going to be of use to you in the longer-term. It would be far too easy today to get yourself involved in things that, with the fullness of time, you will see as being an entire waste.

31 MONDAY   *Moon Age Day 24   Moon Sign Libra*

Almost everything seems to be particularly fulfilling at the moment. Perhaps you now have a greater sense of financial security, or at the very least ideas that can bring it about. You are confident in your ability to do the right thing, but take care to side-step the enquiries of a nosy friend. Enjoy those year-end parties to the full.

GEMINI:
2019 DIARY PAGES

GEMINI:
YOUR YEAR IN BRIEF

Whatever it is you are looking for, there's a reasonable chance you will find at least part of it during January or February. Your chart reveals that you are starting the year with a flourish, so much so that others may struggle to keep up with your pace. Don't let routines irritate you because they are not the most significant part of your life. People from the past could be reappearing now.

March and April continue the generally favourable trends, even if you find that you are being slowed down by situations and influences that are beyond your own control. Get on with jobs you don't want to do as quickly as you can to clear the decks for positive action later. Some surprise visits seem to be in store, particularly from people who have much to teach you. Your love life should also be rewarding.

As the year begins to warm up, May and June could lead to a feeling of inspiration for Gemini, especially professionally. Colleagues may be really listening to what you are saying and following your lead more or less automatically. You may be inclined to hang back socially, but that's only because you don't believe in yourself quite as much as you should and as much as you usually do. Nevertheless there are entertaining possibilities in view later in June.

July and August see you busy as always but now you are probably thinking more in terms of travel than material progress. You remain committed to objectives that have been important to you since the beginning of the year and might even be a little aggressive when it comes to getting what you think is rightfully yours. Just be sure that you don't hurt others on the way and don't take hasty actions that you may come to regret.

As the year grows older and there could be a few decisions that need attention sooner rather than later – although you may not feel inclined to make them. Be decisive during September and October, grasp the nettle and let others know that you mean business. Financially and romantically this should be a good time with things going your way.

The emphasis during November and December is on personal choice. You should be much less susceptible to the influence of others and will find the time and space to do things your own way. November could be the quieter of the two months but December offers variety, changes of scenery and the chance to get together with people you really like but don't see regularly. Any resolutions you make are likely to be followed through quickly next year.

January 2019

1 TUESDAY
Moon Age Day 25   Moon Sign Scorpio

Doing what is expected of you on the first day of the year won't be all that easy this time around. There are a number of planetary positions in your chart that reveal how much you want to be yourself and that means being different. Don't try to shock or outrage others though. It's best to remain cheerful and to explain yourself before you take any action.

2 WEDNESDAY
Moon Age Day 26   Moon Sign Scorpio

Gemini seems to be in a nostalgic mood today, which is fairly unusual for you. Present planetary trends incline you to look back as much as forward and you might see this as being slightly negative. Don't be so sure though. There are lessons to be learned from replaying some situations.

3 THURSDAY
Moon Age Day 27   Moon Sign Sagittarius

Acting on impulse is not to be recommended right now and it would be much better for yourself and all concerned if you take advice from those who know better than you do. Although you really want to push on with specific jobs, it's as if you are walking through treacle. A little patience is called for.

4 FRIDAY
Moon Age Day 28   Moon Sign Sagittarius

Your skill with conversation appears to be highlighted and you should be able to significantly influence colleagues and superiors today. Be prepared to speak your mind, though once again it is important to display a degree of diplomacy if you can manage it.

5 SATURDAY   *Moon Age Day 0   Moon Sign Capricorn*

You are quite outgoing just at the moment but there's nothing particularly unusual about this. What is different is that you are willing to take a little time to stand and stare more. By so doing you get a better appreciation of certain situations than you would by plodding on regardless of anything.

6 SUNDAY   *Moon Age Day 1   Moon Sign Capricorn*

It appears that you are committed to the far distant horizon in a few important issues, which doesn't entirely suit your nature. Immediacy is what you really crave but there are times when you simply have to look ahead. Stave off frustration by taking short periods out today to do whatever takes your fancy.

7 MONDAY   *Moon Age Day 2   Moon Sign Capricorn*

It's the practical issues of life that demand your attention right now and you may have to spend quite a lot of today sorting things out so that you can be comfortable further down the line. Geminis who have been looking for love recently should find today to be quite inspirational. It's time to keep your eyes open.

8 TUESDAY   *Moon Age Day 3   Moon Sign Aquarius*

This is likely to be a time of generally interesting change. Some of these changes will be subtle, whilst others are definite and immediate. None of them bother you in the slightest because you hate life to stand still and you love variety. New friends could be on the way and at least one of them will be a real surprise.

9 WEDNESDAY   *Moon Age Day 4   Moon Sign Aquarius*

It isn't hard to get along with colleagues or even superiors at this stage of the working week and so think about feathering your own nest by putting deliberate effort into making yourself even more popular at work. Socially speaking it won't be necessary because all the attention is coming your way in any case.

10 THURSDAY
Moon Age Day 5   Moon Sign Pisces

Now you ought to be pretty much the centre of attention. Don't be too surprised if you discover you have a secret admirer. This is fine if you are not attached but could be something of an embarrassment otherwise. When it comes to sporting activities, trends suggest that you are likely to be in the winning zone.

11 FRIDAY
Moon Age Day 6   Moon Sign Pisces

For many Geminis, today marks the end of the working week and how pleased you will be that this is the case. The simple fact is that you are tired of doing what you have to and keen to get on with things you like. Your mind is flitting about from one subject to another at the moment and it might be difficult to settle to anything.

12 SATURDAY
Moon Age Day 7   Moon Sign Pisces

It may seem that you have been putting in a lot of time as far as the practicalities of life are concerned and it's true that many of the astrological trends around you now are social in nature. As a result you will want to please yourself today and will most likely be seeking out friends with whom you can have fun.

13 SUNDAY
Moon Age Day 8   Moon Sign Aries

Your social contacts look good and you should find it easy to get on well with just about anyone. Of course there will always be people who don't see life in the way you do but you have the patience to take their opinions on board too. There are times at the moment when your brain is working faster than your hands can keep up.

14 MONDAY
Moon Age Day 9   Moon Sign Aries

As dynamic as ever, you want to make something special of this particular Monday, probably for the sake of your partner or sweetheart if you get the chance. That's fine but do understand that what interests you might not be for them. Before you embark on anything it might be sensible to ask them how they feel.

15 TUESDAY · · · · · · · *Moon Age Day 10 · · Moon Sign Taurus*

There are heart-warming situations cropping up all the time now and you are especially considerate to family members and to your partner in particular. Routines are for the birds this Tuesday because what you want to do the most is to go out and have a good time. Don't be afraid to lay down some ground rules with younger people.

16 WEDNESDAY · · · · · · *Moon Age Day 11 · · Moon Sign Taurus*

You need to keep things as varied and easy-going as you can right now. It could be that you will come across to others as being more forthright than you intend, a situation that you need to watch carefully. Make a joke of serious situations because you will still get your message across.

17 THURSDAY · · · · · · · *Moon Age Day 12 · · Moon Sign Taurus*

Helpful new influences are possible as far as your professional life is concerned. These may offer incentives that were not apparent even a few days ago. Meanwhile you will be in a particularly romantic frame of mind and can find the words of love that are most appropriate to almost any situation.

18 FRIDAY · · · · · · · · · *Moon Age Day 13 · · Moon Sign Gemini*

The Moon is now in your zodiac sign and so therefore very much on your side. Don't take no for an answer either in a professional or a social matter and stick to your guns generally today. Good luck is on your side so you can afford to take the sort of chance you would have shied away from yesterday.

19 SATURDAY · · · · · · · *Moon Age Day 14 · · Moon Sign Gemini*

This should be another generally good day for Gemini but you will need to be just a little diplomatic with people who are not quite as dynamic as you are. Spur of the moment decisions tend to turn out very well and you can certainly turn heads in a romantic sense. This is potentially one of the best days of the month for you.

20 SUNDAY
Moon Age Day 15   Moon Sign Cancer

The more people you mix with at the moment, the greater is your incentive to listen and learn. Gemini is now in a really positive frame of mind and you won't go short of the sort of attention you really love. Remember not to leave really important jobs undone today, especially when you can accomplish so many of them quickly.

21 MONDAY
Moon Age Day 16   Moon Sign Cancer

You are popular at present and liked by almost everyone you come across. However, it's important to realise that you cannot please all of the people all of the time, no matter how much you would wish to do so. There is likely to be at least one person who you find to be over-critical so just accept the fact.

22 TUESDAY
Moon Age Day 17   Moon Sign Leo

There is little doubt about your sense of style right now. You know what looks right, both for yourself and for others – though it's unlikely you can influence those around you quite as much as you might wish. It is also possible that you will start to enjoy the fruits of a regime you have started recently.

23 WEDNESDAY
Moon Age Day 18   Moon Sign Leo

There is no doubt at all about your personal magnetism, which is extremely strong now and noticed by just about everyone you come across. In a professional sense this can give you a distinct edge and could lead to some extra responsibilities coming your way. Make sure that these are going to be rewarded financially.

24 THURSDAY
Moon Age Day 19   Moon Sign Virgo

You need to clear the air over a personal matter that might be slightly spoiling things between yourself and someone close to you in a family sense. Not everyone seems to have your best interests at heart but it is possible you are rather too sensitive for your own good at present. Try to be realistic.

25 FRIDAY
Moon Age Day 20   Moon Sign Virgo

It is gradually becoming obvious that people who refused to listen to your advice in the past are now taking far more notice of you. Maybe this is due to present astrological trends but that isn't the whole reason. You are especially resourceful now in the way you are approaching people generally.

26 SATURDAY
Moon Age Day 21   Moon Sign Libra

You certainly will not be frightened of hard work at this time but there may not be much you need to do on a Saturday if you are not a weekend worker. Instead of searching for jobs unnecessarily, turn your attention to helping others because you are very well equipped to do so at present. Your confidence is not lacking when you need it the most.

27 SUNDAY
Moon Age Day 22   Moon Sign Libra

You can capitalise on the way those around you are behaving at present. If they are reasonable, you co-operate and help to create a formidable team. Should they prove to be awkward, you can refuse to join in and simply prove to the whole world how reasonable you are. It's difficult to lose right now.

28 MONDAY
Moon Age Day 23   Moon Sign Scorpio

Monday is likely to bring a mixed bag and shows you to be in a rather humorous state of mind. That's good because a joke can go a long way towards getting you better known at the moment. There are strong social trends developing so it is unlikely you will be committing yourself exclusively to practical matters.

29 TUESDAY
Moon Age Day 24   Moon Sign Scorpio

Today finds you coming face to face with situations that you might not care for but you should manage to deal with them very easily. What shines out right now is your capabilities, together with the fact that you are enjoying the very experience of life. Friends ought to be very supportive now.

30 WEDNESDAY *Moon Age Day 25   Moon Sign Sagittarius*

It might be the case that you desire a little more peace and quiet today and you can find it by spending more time with family members. Whilst you are doing so it is possible you will be addressing the needs of house and home, which could have been rather ignored of late.

31 THURSDAY *Moon Age Day 26   Moon Sign Sagittarius*

Your ego is getting stronger and so is your desire for adventure. Circumstances might predict that you can't take the risks you would wish and this will probably turn out to be a good thing. The attitude of a friend might need looking at carefully because trends suggest there may be something wrong. Your intuition should tell you how to proceed.

February
2019

1 FRIDAY
Moon Age Day 27   Moon Sign Sagittarius

Now you are keen to get out and about and certainly won't take kindly to being restricted in any way as far as your movements are concerned. The attitude of family members can be something of a puzzle and this might be part of the reason why you are much more likely to be mixing with friends whenever possible.

2 SATURDAY
Moon Age Day 28   Moon Sign Capricorn

All options for change should be considered very carefully and you certainly should not alter things simply for the sake of doing so. Any opportunity to please a loved one should be grasped with both hands, especially if it is someone you have either tended to avoid or inadvertently upset recently.

3 SUNDAY
Moon Age Day 29   Moon Sign Capricorn

Your social life sees newcomers arriving all the time just now and some of them may bring with them a new slant on old situations. Concentrate your efforts where your money is concerned and consider carefully whether the odd little risk is worth taking. There could be something just a little 'bookish' about Gemini this time.

4 MONDAY
Moon Age Day 0   Moon Sign Aquarius

A great deal of energy and enthusiasm is likely to go into your life at the moment and the planetary trends surrounding you are definitely improving significantly. Allow for younger family members to please themselves but keep a watchful eye on them all the same. There's a fine balance to strike in terms of discipline.

5 TUESDAY
Moon Age Day 1   Moon Sign Aquarius

Although you are very good at handing out advice at present, you are not quite so good at receiving it. Perhaps you should think again. There are people around today who really know what they are talking about and who are willing to offer you the benefit of their experience. It's only fair to listen to what they have to say.

6 WEDNESDAY
Moon Age Day 2   Moon Sign Aquarius

It may be hard to keep your mind on a particular subject today, especially if it is something that bores you. You are in the market for enjoyment and will want to join forces with people who have a similar view. Don't forget your family responsibilities but there are ways of incorporating these into your social needs.

7 THURSDAY
Moon Age Day 3   Moon Sign Pisces

Creating an agreeable atmosphere is part of what matters to you now. You are almost certain to be making new friends but at the same time hearth and home prove to be extremely important. Someone you know well could be making some sort of professional offer that you will find hard to refuse.

8 FRIDAY
Moon Age Day 4   Moon Sign Pisces

There is likely to be a good deal of financial stability in your life right now, which isn't always the case for your zodiac sign. Many Geminis will be feeling quite mellow and might be taking notice of situations they would ignore under normal circumstances. Creating a positive atmosphere amongst friends seems important in your chart now.

9 SATURDAY
Moon Age Day 5   Moon Sign Aries

Financial stability is more than possible under present planetary trends and there is a good chance you will be keeping more of what you earn at this time. Friends may tend to be quite demanding today but they do have your best interests at heart, which ought to be pleasing. Meanwhile, family life should be steady.

10 SUNDAY

Moon Age Day 6   Moon Sign Aries

Although there is a slight tendency to think about number one at this time, this is something you will overcome because your compassion is strong. You will be very loyal to your friends and are inclined to go that extra mile on their behalf. Romance is likely to throw up some interesting possibilities now.

11 MONDAY

Moon Age Day 7   Moon Sign Aries

A very self-assured and quite dynamic Gemini is likely to greet today. Things ought to be looking fairly good for you at the moment, even if you have a tendency to worry about nothing in particular. Whatever you do in a professional or practical sense today, it's important to go for gold.

12 TUESDAY

Moon Age Day 8   Moon Sign Taurus

Peace and quiet just doesn't appeal to you at this stage of the week and the more so because there have been quite a few restrictions placed around you in the past few months. Some Geminis will be very keen to paint the town red this evening but make sure you are not spending money you don't have.

13 WEDNESDAY

Moon Age Day 9   Moon Sign Taurus

There are times when as a Gemini you are inclined to speak without thinking as much as you might. This leads to numerous apologies but can be avoided altogether now if you use a little tact and diplomacy. Amongst friends your popularity remains generally high and your social prospects are good.

14 THURSDAY

Moon Age Day 10   Moon Sign Gemini

Anything out of the box, unusual or curious is bound to fascinate you right now. There is likely to be good news on the way and you can expect a red-letter day in a general sense. You throw all your energy into things and it would be very easy for you to cope with a dozen different matters at the same time.

15 FRIDAY
Moon Age Day 11   Moon Sign Gemini

Your good luck looks set to continue and it should be easy to be in the right place to make significant gains. People actively encourage you to speak your mind – not that you take all that much persuasion. Your dealings are all above-board and the amount of trust coming your way is noteworthy. Your popularity should also be high.

16 SATURDAY
Moon Age Day 12   Moon Sign Cancer

Don't be shy today. People are watching you and it is important for you to shine. This is especially true at work, but you can't rule out the possibility of some romantic admirers coming your way too! There may be some small gains to be made financially, but you will have to keep your eyes open if you are going to notice them.

17 SUNDAY
Moon Age Day 13   Moon Sign Cancer

This is a very forgiving day and one during which you will show great care and compassion for others, which is, after all, only your real nature shining through. There is also a good deal of concern coming your way, sometimes from directions that could be particularly surprising.

18 MONDAY
Moon Age Day 14   Moon Sign Leo

You are likely to be slightly more liberal with money now and probably with good cause. Although you could be quieter than usual today, you will recognise a bargain when you see one and won't be tardy when it comes to snapping it up. For this reason alone, you will be in a mood for shopping.

19 TUESDAY
Moon Age Day 15   Moon Sign Leo

Don't be too quick to jump to conclusions right now. You are still inclined to believe you have all the answers, but you won't have a huge amount of good fortune to back up your hunches. As a result, it would be sensible to seek sound advice and to give all matters a lot of careful thought.

20 WEDNESDAY *Moon Age Day 16 Moon Sign Virgo*

Out here in the middle of the week, Saturday and Sunday seem a mile away. You feel you are running out of steam, and yet some of your actions show just how much energy you can have if you get on with things. The fact is that you are only at your best right now when doing things that have some particular fascination for you.

21 THURSDAY *Moon Age Day 17 Moon Sign Virgo*

There are many different ways to do the same job and you seem to be trying all of them now. Don't allow yourself to become bored, or to be tied down with things you simply 'have' to do, that you fail to create the necessary space for innovation and spontaneous action.

22 FRIDAY *Moon Age Day 18 Moon Sign Libra*

While you might not get everything you 'want' today, you already have much of what you need. You could also be coming up with some ingenious ideas to make the most of the hand that life has dealt you. By this afternoon, you will be looking for new incentives and finding the right people to offer them to.

23 SATURDAY *Moon Age Day 19 Moon Sign Libra*

The weekend brings a burst of enthusiasm for a subject that might not have played any particular part in your life up to now. Ringing the changes is very important for Gemini, especially so at the moment. Care and attention to details in any sphere of your life is likely to pay handsome dividends later.

24 SUNDAY *Moon Age Day 20 Moon Sign Scorpio*

You can expect this Sunday to be entertaining, and perhaps also to give you the opportunity to explore the true depths of a romantic attachment. You could find your desire for to get out and about stifled by circumstance but you must not allow this to get you down. There are always alternatives and some of them are exciting.

25 MONDAY
Moon Age Day 21   Moon Sign Scorpio

Rather than looking for something new in your life, especially in terms of your career, it would probably be better today to consolidate what you have. If people are unsure of your motives and intentions, now is the time to put them in the picture. By the evening, you may well be ready for a fling with friends.

26 TUESDAY
Moon Age Day 22   Moon Sign Sagittarius

You could find yourself amongst family and friends at the moment but with the lunar low around you will probably also be quite pleased to spend some time alone. This is certainly not the most progressive or positive part of February for you but there will be the chance to think and plan ahead.

27 WEDNESDAY
Moon Age Day 23   Moon Sign Sagittarius

You are in a good position to influence the way others think, even if you don't necessarily have what it takes to get ahead yourself. One area of life that does look quite good is romance and there ought to be a chance to impress someone at work, even if it is unintentional.

28 THURSDAY
Moon Age Day 24   Moon Sign Sagittarius

This is a day when you won't take kindly to being told what to do. Remember to be tolerant of others and not to blame the messenger if instructions come along that don't please you, especially if that person is only following the orders they have been given. It isn't like Gemini to be resentful, but there is a danger you could be now.

♊ March 2019

1 FRIDAY
Moon Age Day 25   Moon Sign Capricorn

Now you have more energy and a greater sense of purpose in your physical activity. Gemini at its best begins to show and you will be able to express yourself in the most positive way. This will gain you more popularity, which is often reward enough itself to the Twins.

2 SATURDAY
Moon Age Day 26   Moon Sign Capricorn

The odd and unusual in life now becomes your main focus. Perhaps the secret parts of the Gemini mind are now on show? You are often accused of being superficial but this isn't true at all. On the other hand, when you look into the darkest recesses of your mind you may not find this too comfortable and might decide to keep the lid in place anyway.

3 SUNDAY
Moon Age Day 27   Moon Sign Aquarius

You are less introspective now and more inclined to share your ideas and opinions with the world at large, whether or not the world wants to listen. Renewed optimism might find you taking up a plan you abandoned some time ago. You are older and wiser now and can see things more clearly.

4 MONDAY
Moon Age Day 28   Moon Sign Aquarius

Monday should find you anxious to experience something new. Feeding the senses is important to your zodiac sign and you won't stop once you have set out on any sort of quest. You may be feeling somewhat haunted by a few odd occurrences in your life, though they fascinate you rather than being a worry.

5 TUESDAY
Moon Age Day 29   Moon Sign Aquarius

Your capacity for work is extremely good at the moment and you shouldn't have any difficulty at all doing several jobs at the same time. The problem is that no matter how much you do, there is always something else waiting in the wings. Energetic as you are, you will have to call a halt eventually.

6 WEDNESDAY ☿
Moon Age Day 0   Moon Sign Pisces

Any clouds that do appear today should have significant silver linings. It is important to look beyond any specific event, into the reason for it. Once you do this, you have a better understanding and can react more sensibly. There could be a quite a few compliments coming your way, most likely this evening.

7 THURSDAY ☿
Moon Age Day 1   Moon Sign Pisces

The practical side of your nature is clearly on display today and it appears you can get plenty done out there in the real world. Moves to alter situations at work might meet some resistance at first but you are unlikely to be diverted from your chosen course of action. Remain diplomatic whenever possible.

8 FRIDAY ☿
Moon Age Day 2   Moon Sign Aries

The end of the working week ought to find you being very set in your views. Not everyone will agree with what you have to say and it won't be possible to bully your way through. When situations threaten to get out of hand it might be sensible to bring in a neutral third party.

9 SATURDAY ☿
Moon Age Day 3   Moon Sign Aries

Saturday brings a slightly quieter period, at least where material matters are concerned. When it comes to casual conversations, it seems you are as bright and chatty as ever. There is a distinct possibility you find it a little difficult to take anything all that seriously between now and Monday.

10 SUNDAY ☿ *Moon Age Day 4   Moon Sign Taurus*

Sunday finds you willing to enjoy some quality time in a family sense and you will probably be far less motivated to achieve material objectives. Those jobs that seem like a perpetual sausage machine should be left completely alone if possible today, allowing for a temporary change of emphasis.

11 MONDAY ☿ *Moon Age Day 5   Moon Sign Taurus*

Try your very best not to be constantly on the defensive today. This can be a slightly prickly time for Gemini. The most likely reason for this is that you suspect you are not being completely trusted. It is just possible that there is a degree of paranoia around right now – coming from your direction.

12 TUESDAY ☿ *Moon Age Day 6   Moon Sign Taurus*

There are many different forms of progress in the average life and you are looking for all of them at the same time today. Certainly you should find yourself more in charge in professional situations, whilst when it comes to co-operative ventures, you clearly want to be in the driving seat.

13 WEDNESDAY ☿ *Moon Age Day 7   Moon Sign Gemini*

The middle of the week finds the Moon in your zodiac sign. This means that you are in for some good luck and that you can exploit situations much more successfully. The lunar high should also ensure that the reaction you get from others is both positive and reassuring.

14 THURSDAY ☿ *Moon Age Day 8   Moon Sign Gemini*

It is very unlikely that today will bring any slowing of the general pace of your life. On the contrary, you need to be active and won't stay still for more than a few minutes at a time. Seek to increase your personal influence generally but spend some time with your loved ones, particularly your partner.

15 FRIDAY ☿ *Moon Age Day 9 Moon Sign Cancer*

The middle of the month is already here and if there is something you want to do but have been putting off, now is the time to get on with it. Your popularity is likely to be high, so you can also ask for a few favours and expect your requests to be looked at fairly. Don't commit yourself to ventures that don't interest you.

16 SATURDAY ☿ *Moon Age Day 10 Moon Sign Cancer*

There is a strong emphasis on communication today and it is very important to make sure that you are getting your message across as successfully as you can. Focus on doing one job at a time today, instead of the hundred you normally take on. It is important to specialise at the moment.

17 SUNDAY ☿ *Moon Age Day 11 Moon Sign Cancer*

If you find that you are impatient with practical matters, it is either because you are bored with them or simply that you need a change of scene. Do what you must today in order to feel more satisfied with life but beware of making any rash decisions when it comes to finances. It would be easy to lose money under present trends.

18 MONDAY ☿ *Moon Age Day 12 Moon Sign Leo*

A charming and easy-going manner is something you have in abundance this Monday and this can be turned to your advantage with no trouble whatsoever. Take those you care for by surprise and also be ready to make some new friends at some stage during the day. Gemini is on a social roll at this time.

19 TUESDAY ☿ *Moon Age Day 13 Moon Sign Leo*

Domestic issues now appear to be very rewarding. This is partly because you have so much time for people at home and won't be quite so inclined as you often are to dash off at a moment's notice. People are especially fond of you and they tend to show it a great deal, sometimes to the point of causing a little embarrassment.

20 WEDNESDAY ☿   *Moon Age Day 14*   *Moon Sign Virgo*

Pace yourself and work according to plans you laid down some time ago, rather than trying to make up the rules as you go along. It's important that others know the way you are likely to react, in which case they will help you out. Most Geminis will relish all the support they can get during this twenty-four hours.

21 THURSDAY ☿   *Moon Age Day 15*   *Moon Sign Virgo*

You need to set yourself some realistic deadlines if you are going to achieve as much as you can now. The potential for mixing business with pleasure is great, so Geminis who are working today might be the luckiest. You can really make an impression when it counts the most and that gets you noticed even more than usual.

22 FRIDAY ☿   *Moon Age Day 16*   *Moon Sign Libra*

You will have plenty of chance to let your light shine today, no matter what you choose to do. Slowly but surely the planets are lining up to allow you a more positive approach, while general good luck is going to be a bigger part of the scenario than has been the case for the last few days.

23 SATURDAY ☿   *Moon Age Day 17*   *Moon Sign Libra*

Unfortunately you can expect some minor setbacks in terms of your career, but these are nothing you can't sort out quite easily at a later date. Part of the problem is that it is quite difficult to focus your mind on practical and material matters just now. There is a slightly wistful quality to Gemini at the moment that can come as a shock.

24 SUNDAY ☿   *Moon Age Day 18*   *Moon Sign Scorpio*

A livelier period now comes along and Sunday brings change and diversity to the lives of most Geminis. There are almost certainly some gains to be made, mostly by showing what a cheerful and optimistic individual you really are. Just remember, more haste and less speed is the pattern you are looking for.

25 MONDAY ☿ *Moon Age Day 19* *Moon Sign Scorpio*

Your mind is both quick and sharp, with a biting wit that can catch almost anyone off guard. Most of what you say goes right to the mark but this might mean that you upset one or two people without realising it. If you keep your level of sarcasm down to about half what it can be, things should work out fine.

26 TUESDAY ☿ *Moon Age Day 20* *Moon Sign Sagittarius*

This is not a day for jumping to conclusions, or for taking prohibitive actions of any sort. Sit and watch life go by, rather than trying to become too involved in it. The more you are willing to rest and recuperate, the better will be your readiness when the lunar low passes away by Thursday.

27 WEDNESDAY ☿ *Moon Age Day 21* *Moon Sign Sagittarius*

You can find plenty of enjoyment today if you look for it, though it is hardly likely to be of the most adventurous sort. Stay reasonably quiet and observe the way others are behaving. As steady as this period might be, it offers more potential to make gains later than almost any other time this month.

28 THURSDAY ☿ *Moon Age Day 22* *Moon Sign Capricorn*

Your personal charm can make a big impact on almost anyone right now and you will be less inclined to get on the wrong side of people. Warm and sincere in your attitude, your desire to get involved in charitable pursuits is that much stronger and with you on board almost any enterprise is heading for success.

29 FRIDAY *Moon Age Day 23* *Moon Sign Capricorn*

Wonderful social events can be on the way but you may have to sort out a minor disaster at home or amongst friends before this can be the case. You adapt quickly and think well on your feet. These are the hallmarks of Gemini and they are certainly on display at the moment and for some days to come.

30 SATURDAY   *Moon Age Day 24   Moon Sign Capricorn*

An important discussion might fail to bring you exactly what you want, which will go down hard after a few days during which you have become used to getting your own way. Some compromise might be necessary and could actually lead to a greater measure of success than you were originally hoping for.

31 SUNDAY   *Moon Age Day 25   Moon Sign Aquarius*

A sense of duty and responsibility, never really that high on the Twins' list of priorities, is practically nonexistent at the moment. Today is for having a good time, which is something you do understand only too well. Look out for new enterprises and methods of turning a good time into ways of making extra cash.

April

2019

1 MONDAY
Moon Age Day 26   Moon Sign Aquarius

It is the good things that others are saying about you that sets you apart right now and this should make for a very positive sort of day all round. Comfortable and able to make a better impression than was the case earlier in the year, you are likely to push ahead strongly with both existing and new plans.

2 TUESDAY
Moon Age Day 27   Moon Sign Pisces

The focus right now is on practical matters. Business and career are now clearly to the fore and you are raring to go. Most Geminis have the gift of the gab when it comes to sales, and you are no exception in this regard at the moment. Your creative potential is very good and you just instinctively know when something looks right.

3 WEDNESDAY
Moon Age Day 28   Moon Sign Pisces

You have a need for fun and enjoyment and you want to enjoy the lighter side of life if you possibly can. Although you might be fairly committed to practical projects at this stage of the week you can afford to take at least some time out to please yourself. If family arrangements seem over-complicated to you, simplify them.

4 THURSDAY
Moon Age Day 29   Moon Sign Pisces

You seem highly motivated and have lots of energy for improving your personal surroundings or life situation in general. The only trouble is that little things keep going wrong. Not everyone you know is equally helpful and, all in all, you will need to wait for tomorrow before things improve noticeably.

5 FRIDAY
Moon Age Day 0   Moon Sign Aries

New friendships are likely to emerge at any time and you take well to new situations. Try to avoid working hard to push yourself into a position that you don't really want. There are times when the grass looks greener on the other side of the fence, but the truth is that it is probably more worn than the lawn you are standing on now.

6 SATURDAY
Moon Age Day 1   Moon Sign Aries

You need some variety this weekend and any form of journey would suit you down to the ground. Conforming to the expectations of others won't always be quite as easy as you might wish but you do have what it takes to bring others round to your point of view. When it comes to the gift of the gab you are second to none.

7 SUNDAY
Moon Age Day 2   Moon Sign Taurus

You could feel that some personal progress is lacking today but bearing in mind that this is Sunday in any case, you probably won't be too worried. The time is right to have fun and you will be quite prepared to do whatever it takes to persuade others to let their hair down and to join in with you.

8 MONDAY
Moon Age Day 3   Moon Sign Taurus

There is something very restless about you this Monday and you won't be all that happy to stand and stare when you could be getting involved in any situation. Sporting Geminis do very well under current trends, and there are gains to be made in home-based issues. Stay away from pointless rules and regulations that will only annoy you.

9 TUESDAY
Moon Age Day 4   Moon Sign Gemini

New initiatives are definitely up your street at the moment and you can afford to push your luck a little now. This is a time to show the world what you are capable of achieving and you won't want to waste a second of what looks like a particularly interesting and productive time.

10 WEDNESDAY   *Moon Age Day 5   Moon Sign Gemini*

You tend to be fairly forceful in the way you speak right now but that is quite understandable when you are on such a roll. You have great mental energy and a personality that just can't be bettered. Despite the fact that you could be just a little boastful, it is quite obvious that you are much loved.

11 THURSDAY   *Moon Age Day 6   Moon Sign Gemini*

This is a day during which you definitely do need to please yourself and you won't take at all kindly to being told what to do by anyone. It ought to be more than possible to enchant your partner at the moment and if you have been looking for new love recently, now is the time to concentrate most of your efforts.

12 FRIDAY   *Moon Age Day 7   Moon Sign Cancer*

Once again you are inclined to speak your mind, but there is nothing remotely strange about that state of affairs. Something you want to happen in the near future is definitely in the balance right now. Since there is nothing you can do about it, however, the best thing to do is nothing. Worrying won't help.

13 SATURDAY   *Moon Age Day 8   Moon Sign Cancer*

Certain elements of your personal life could prove to be a little difficult right now and you should heed the planets' advice to be quite circumspect before you wade into anything complicated that might upset the applecart. It may be that your partner or sweetheart has been listening to gossip but leave matters alone because they should resolve themselves.

14 SUNDAY   *Moon Age Day 9   Moon Sign Leo*

A quieter and more reflective Gemini is in evidence right now. With this slightly less hectic spell comes a time to reflect and to look back at the way past situations have a bearing on your present life. Romance is once again favoured but you might need to be a little stern with a wayward family member.

15 MONDAY
Moon Age Day 10   Moon Sign Leo

Your ego is boosted at just the right time and you find that your popularity is extremely high around now. Something you are presently looking forward to is probably going to take a little more work than you expected so it is important to keep your head down until matters are settled.

16 TUESDAY
Moon Age Day 11   Moon Sign Virgo

You might be thinking a good deal at the moment about personal security. In addition, there is more scepticism about you than is usually the case for Gemini. It might be best to make certain you don't get things out of proportion because you work best when you remain trusting and open-minded.

17 WEDNESDAY
Moon Age Day 12   Moon Sign Virgo

Stay away from rules and regulations as much as you can because it is clear that you don't take well to them for the moment. The fact is that you want to do everything your own way, which is fine on those occasions when you know what you are doing. You have plenty to say for yourself in social situations.

18 THURSDAY
Moon Age Day 13   Moon Sign Libra

This is a time when relationships can prove to be very useful in a number of ways. There are gains to be made in your finances, probably by discussing plans with those closest to you. New incentives at work make this part of the week potentially very interesting and quite varied.

19 FRIDAY
Moon Age Day 14   Moon Sign Libra

The things you learn from colleagues or friends are of great use to you now. Keep your ears wide open and don't turn down well-meant advice, simply because it comes from a rather dubious source. The fact is that you are allowing the suspicious side of your nature too much control and this is never a good idea.

20 SATURDAY   *Moon Age Day 15   Moon Sign Scorpio*

Take a break from routines, even weekend ones. The year is advancing and you should be feeling the need to spread your wings. Perhaps you might consider a trip out somewhere? If you do, make certain you have someone along with you who is entertaining and who you always like to have around.

21 SUNDAY   *Moon Age Day 16   Moon Sign Scorpio*

You might have to get rid of something that has outlived its usefulness today and, if so, try to avoid the unnecessary nostalgia that usually accompanies such situations in your case. Friends are ready to offer you timely advice, though the planets suggest that the truth is you have more to impart to them than they have to you.

22 MONDAY   *Moon Age Day 17   Moon Sign Sagittarius*

You might have to put a plan or two to one side for the next couple of days whilst the lunar low is around. Opt for a simpler sort of life if you can and be willing to let others take some of the strain. You will want to put your thinking head on later in the week but don't actually take on any more than you have to right now.

23 TUESDAY   *Moon Age Day 18   Moon Sign Sagittarius*

Not everything is likely to go the way you would wish as far as your finances are concerned and you will need to take care not to spend more than you can reasonably afford for the moment. With a distinct lack of lustre today you won't be shining in social situations as much as would usually be the case.

24 WEDNESDAY *Moon Age Day 19   Moon Sign Capricorn*

This is likely to be a day of preparation and involves you looking carefully at all eventualities before you decide to move in any specific direction. Keep an eye open if you are going to the shops. There are bargains around at present and you are in just the right frame of mind to snap some of them up.

25 THURSDAY *Moon Age Day 20 Moon Sign Capricorn*

There is a good chance that you can turn an interest into a lucrative sideline now. Spend some time thinking about this, as you career through another busy day. Geminis always make the most of every minute, despite the fact that you have a lazy streak. A diversion in the direction of luxury later in the day could appeal to you.

26 FRIDAY *Moon Age Day 21 Moon Sign Capricorn*

Ready for a change, and champing at the bit to get away from anything tedious or routine, you need to talk to family members and friends about holidays. If you could manage an immediate change of scene, so much the better. If not, the travel will have to be in your mind for the moment.

27 SATURDAY *Moon Age Day 22 Moon Sign Aquarius*

Your ambitions are fired up, which can be something of a downer if you don't work on a Saturday and can therefore not charge ahead with practical plans. You need to control your temper, even if at times you feel yourself to be pushed into a corner. If you remain calm, cool and collected, you are certain to win through.

28 SUNDAY *Moon Age Day 23 Moon Sign Aquarius*

Rest and relaxation would be good, though you are unlikely to get much of either today. In a sense, it's your own fault. The fact is that you have been proving yourself so well in every area of late, someone always wants to pick your brains. At some stage during the day, you need to reserve an hour or two just for you.

29 MONDAY *Moon Age Day 24 Moon Sign Pisces*

Socially speaking today brings a breath of fresh air into your life. There are new people around, many of whom you will find extremely interesting. Amongst the new acquaintances you meet, look out for other people born under the same your own zodiac sign as you as you may feel a natural affinity with them.

30 TUESDAY   *Moon Age Day 25   Moon Sign Pisces*

Not everyone wants to listen to what you are saying, but since you can't force them to do so, there really isn't too much point in pushing issues. Instead, you need to think long and hard about the social aspects of your life, maybe thinking about taking up a new hobby, or somehow passing your present skills to others.

8 May
II
2019

1 WEDNESDAY
Moon Age Day 26   Moon Sign Pisces

If you get the chance to travel now, you should certainly do so. A change of scene would suit your present mood wonderfully, the more so if you are in the company of people you like a great deal and who you find stimulating. What you don't need today is to be stuck in the same old rut.

2 THURSDAY
Moon Age Day 27   Moon Sign Aries

You benefit a great deal today from mixing with as broad a cross-section of people as possible. This is a sociable time and one during which you might also be turning your mind towards matters of love and romance. Financial problems can be addressed successfully, particularly with the help of family members.

3 FRIDAY
Moon Age Day 28   Moon Sign Aries

A more light-hearted time socially and for your love life allows you to think about getting out into the bright lights. Certainly you won't take too kindly to being cooped up in the same place all the time and you need the intellectual stimulus that comes from mixing with intelligent and thoughtful types.

4 SATURDAY
Moon Age Day 0   Moon Sign Taurus

You may have your work cut out trying to make personal relationships turn out exactly as you would wish. You may feel that it is other people who are awkward at present and who simply will not adopt what you see as being a rational point of view. It might be best to surround yourself with friends for the moment.

5 SUNDAY
Moon Age Day 1   Moon Sign Taurus

The forces of change are in operation. The present position of the Sun makes it both necessary and desirable to get rid of aspects of life that are not serving you well now. This might mean a change of job for some Geminis, or perhaps thoughts of an alteration in your living circumstances.

6 MONDAY
Moon Age Day 2   Moon Sign Taurus

You are anxious to broaden your horizons in just about any way possible. Romance is beckoning for many people born under the sign of the Twins and the start of a new week offers new chances to make a good impression. Don't be surprised if you feel a little off colour early today.

7 TUESDAY
Moon Age Day 3   Moon Sign Gemini

Rely on your intuitive insight, which is suddenly strong as the Moon surges into your zodiac sign. When the lunar high comes along in the spring, the prognosis has to be excellent. All you must remember today is that you won't make full use of your potential sitting around and doing nothing.

8 WEDNESDAY
Moon Age Day 4   Moon Sign Gemini

What an excellent time this would be for putting the finishing touch to fresh and innovative ideas. With determination you can overthrow obstacles that might normally get in your way. Your confidence levels remain generally high and it is clear that you have a number of agendas at present.

9 THURSDAY
Moon Age Day 5   Moon Sign Cancer

Although you are eager for professional success, things may not be turning out quite the way you would wish. Take life steadily and look for opportunities in places where other people fail to see them. You have inner confidence, but this lies buried beneath the surface for most of the day and you will need reassurance.

10 FRIDAY · · · · · · · · · · · · · · · *Moon Age Day 6   Moon Sign Cancer*

There are newer and broader horizons on offer now, even if you fail to notice them early in the day. People you don't know particularly well appear to have a much better understanding of you than you may have realised, and it could be hard to see right through to the heart of some matters in the way you normally do easily.

11 SATURDAY · · · · · · · · · · · · · · · *Moon Age Day 7   Moon Sign Leo*

Although you are willing to meet with people today and quite able to speak your mind, for some reason things still will not go entirely your way. Be patient, keep your cool and don't react to provocation. Remember these pieces of advice and you are certain to win through in the end.

12 SUNDAY · · · · · · · · · · · · · · · *Moon Age Day 8   Moon Sign Leo*

You are on a continued high with regard to intellectual interests of almost any sort. Be willing to look again at old issues that return to your life, though your attitude to them this time around is likely to be quite different from before. Money matters should be easier to deal with and you could find cash coming from unexpected places.

13 MONDAY · · · · · · · · · · · · · · · *Moon Age Day 9   Moon Sign Virgo*

There ought to be great co-operation at home, even from younger people, one or two of whom might have been going through a rebellious streak in the recent past. If you can't get what you want at work by simply asking, some more drastic – though probably funny – solution may be necessary.

14 TUESDAY · · · · · · · · · · · · · · · *Moon Age Day 10   Moon Sign Virgo*

You won't get what you want from this day if you allow your impatience to show too much. Remember that people around you see your actions so your attitude is very important. Even when you feel frustrated by circumstances, you need to smile and to maintain a state of equilibrium.

15 WEDNESDAY
Moon Age Day 11   Moon Sign Libra

This is an excellent time to emphasise your practical skills and to show the world in general that you are very capable. Gemini is also very realistic in its attitude and approach right now. This makes it easy for you to accept life the way it is and therefore to start your thinking from a reasonable platform.

16 THURSDAY
Moon Age Day 12   Moon Sign Libra

Your finances should improve as you attract the goodwill of influential people. You can thank the present planetary line-up for this state of affairs. It also helps you to create a stable and satisfying period with regard to love and romance, without an over-sentimental attitude.

17 FRIDAY
Moon Age Day 13   Moon Sign Scorpio

With goodwill from others and a little extra effort on your part, today could be better than average. However, you are likely to notice that some of your efforts fall on stony ground and the only way to get round the problems is to wait until tomorrow. More effort than is wise will only tire you.

18 SATURDAY
Moon Age Day 14   Moon Sign Scorpio

You seem to be quite ready for a change and will seek this out at every possible opportunity right now. Perhaps you are tired with the way your professional life is going and want to alter things somewhat? No matter how you look at situations, they seem to gain from a significant shake-up.

19 SUNDAY
Moon Age Day 15   Moon Sign Scorpio

Given the right social circumstances, and of course the best sort of audience, you can make an excellent impression at the moment. If you are a Sunday worker, expect superiors to be watching you closely, albeit in a positive way. Keep abreast of local news – you may have to act on it.

20 MONDAY *Moon Age Day 16   Moon Sign Sagittarius*

Think about a temporary break from responsibilities and allow others to take the strain just now. Take some time out to indulge the pleasure seeking qualities within your own nature, if you can, and enjoy a little luxury in your life. A visit to a sauna or perhaps a relaxing massage would represent the best of all worlds to you now.

21 TUESDAY *Moon Age Day 17   Moon Sign Sagittarius*

Practical matters appear to be beyond your ability to control on this particular Tuesday. This being the case, there isn't too much point in trying. Opt for a social sort of day and one during which you get to chat freely with as many different people at possible. Look up someone you haven't seen for a while.

22 WEDNESDAY *Moon Age Day 18   Moon Sign Capricorn*

As trends move on, you can now go a long way towards achieving your objectives and won't be stuck for something to do once the professional day is over either. Although some small obstacles to success are obvious in your chart at present, these merely act to further stimulate your efforts.

23 THURSDAY *Moon Age Day 19   Moon Sign Capricorn*

You are sharp and insightful now, and there is much to be gained from capitalising on these traits. Look at people carefully, especially if you are going to need to trust them to do something for you. What your instincts tell you about them will give you all the information you need.

24 FRIDAY *Moon Age Day 20   Moon Sign Aquarius*

You really should have some ambitious projects up and running by now and if this isn't the case it's time to get your skates on. Not everyone is equally helpful today but the people who count the most are going to be on your side and remain there through thick and thin. A particularly good friend might need your advice.

25 SATURDAY   *Moon Age Day 21   Moon Sign Aquarius*

Some of the routines of life should prove far more rewarding than you might have expected today. In a confident mood, you should have many friends around who will do all they can to help you along. Some of the drudgery is taken out of jobs you don't care for, possibly because pals are lending a hand.

26 SUNDAY   *Moon Age Day 22   Moon Sign Aquarius*

Someone from your past is likely to make a return visit to your life around this time. With renewed determination for a project that you might have thought was dead in the water some time ago, it looks as though you are proving your experience and capability now.

27 MONDAY   *Moon Age Day 23   Moon Sign Pisces*

It is necessary at the start of this week to commit yourself fully to the task in hand and to defer some of the pleasures until later. A slight conflict inside your own mind could be the result and only by tapping into your most patient qualities can you push ahead progressively, without becoming sidetracked.

28 TUESDAY   *Moon Age Day 24   Moon Sign Pisces*

Much of today should be wonderful if spent in the bosom of your family. Of course, if this is a working day for you, it is likely your domestic bliss won't start until the evening. That doesn't matter because it's the quality of what relationships have to offer that counts far more than the amount of time.

29 WEDNESDAY   *Moon Age Day 25   Moon Sign Aries*

There is knowledge around for Gemini now and this doesn't simply extend to recognition of how to get things done. You seem to be looking into the very heart of life and as a result find yourself a good deal wiser. It won't take long for those around you to realise that you are the best source of honest advice.

30 THURSDAY
Moon Age Day 26   Moon Sign Aries

There may be a few objectives that you cannot address, if only because you aren't a machine and need rest from time to time. Worldly achievement need not be your number one consideration today and there is a more introspective phase getting in the way. Spend an hour or two alone if you can.

31 FRIDAY
Moon Age Day 27   Moon Sign Aries

This may be an interval during which you are partly rethinking your life and the direction you are taking. This trend is mixed with the excitement you feel at being able to spread your wings. Spend as much time as you can in the company of people who really know how to party.

June

2019

1 SATURDAY
Moon Age Day 28   Moon Sign Taurus

Practical issues seem to be your number one priority today, mainly because you have been avoiding them for a few days. Your powers of communication should be better and there should be a chance to put right something that has been an issue in your life for weeks. Family trends look positive and happy.

2 SUNDAY
Moon Age Day 29   Moon Sign Taurus

You have plenty of get up and go today, which is just as well because it is likely that there is much to be done. Keep abreast of local news and events, at the same time look carefully at the 'big picture' regarding your own life. A personal touch to congratulations in the family would be appreciated.

3 MONDAY
Moon Age Day 0   Moon Sign Gemini

The lunar high is back, which is particularly auspicious at the start of a new week. You can race around and get masses of jobs done, clearing the decks for action that comes along later. If you are making anything, use the best possible materials you can find. Quality is what you demand and find when your drive is so strong.

4 TUESDAY
Moon Age Day 1   Moon Sign Gemini

You still know exactly what you want from life and should not have too much trouble getting it. Turning your attention away from the practical aspects of life, this is a period when you will be concentrating more on simply having a good time. Back your hunches, and look out for a small financial advantage coming along that you didn't expect.

5 WEDNESDAY   *Moon Age Day 2   Moon Sign Cancer*

There is a tendency for pressure to upset your judgement today, which is why you have to approach all situations slowly and steadily, and avoid over-reacting to anything. Not everyone seems to be on your side, but when the chips are down there are a number of friends upon whom you can rely.

6 THURSDAY   *Moon Age Day 3   Moon Sign Cancer*

There is no doubt that you prefer to live for the moment – that's pretty much the attitude of all the Air signs. However, you also have a realisation that some prior planning is necessary, a fact that certainly is not lost on you today. Maintain a sense of proportion regarding a tiff that could ensue later in the day.

7 FRIDAY   *Moon Age Day 4   Moon Sign Leo*

Maintaining a high profile is likely to lead to some positive meetings today, both professionally and on a purely social level. Once again, you find yourself beset by the need to move around and if you haven't managed much travel yet this year, the call of fresh fields and pastures new is difficult to resist.

8 SATURDAY   *Moon Age Day 5   Moon Sign Leo*

Be careful before you say yes today, especially to people you don't know well. You need to look with great attention at documents and particularly at bargains that look too good to be true. It looks highly likely that they are not all they seem. All in all, it might be best not to spend any money at all, unless you are on very sure ground.

9 SUNDAY   *Moon Age Day 6   Moon Sign Virgo*

Smooth and steady progress could set this Sunday apart, whether or not you are a weekend worker. If you are not committed to practical matters, you would respond very well now to a trip into the past. Should you want to feed your intellectual curiosity and your sense of nostalgia perhaps try a museum or an art gallery.

10 MONDAY
Moon Age Day 7   Moon Sign Virgo

Look out for a boost in professional matters, perhaps even a change of job for some Geminis. You won't find everyone equally helpful because there is a degree of competition around at present. You have what it takes to rise above petty jealousies and should not take too much notice of any teasing that is going on.

11 TUESDAY
Moon Age Day 8   Moon Sign Virgo

Being in the know is as easy as looking into the face of the people you are associating with at present. Your intuition is extremely strong and the chance of anyone deliberately misleading you now is virtually nil. There is just the slightest chance of unnecessary little mishaps, however, so watch your step.

12 WEDNESDAY
Moon Age Day 9   Moon Sign Libra

Not everyone you know will be equally helpful today, though perhaps they have their reasons for this, and it ought to be easy to guess the situation once you do a little digging. Your confidence is high and the need to make changes in and around your home is likely to be fairly strong all day.

13 THURSDAY
Moon Age Day 10   Moon Sign Libra

If you are going to appear on a public platform, the chances are you will spend ages preparing yourself. That's fine, but remember that the spontaneous quality of Gemini is also important. There isn't a sign of the zodiac that can 'busk it' better than yours can. If you don't believe this to be true, ask a friend.

14 FRIDAY
Moon Age Day 11   Moon Sign Scorpio

There is a definite chance you could end up in pointless disputes today which would be a pity, especially at a time when there is so much else to do. Of course, it takes two to tango and if you refuse to join in, no argument can take place at all. Simply don't rise to any bait, no matter how provocative it seems to be.

15 SATURDAY   *Moon Age Day 12   Moon Sign Scorpio*

If there is one fact you can rely up on today, it is that you will keep busy. With a thousand things to be done and only you to address them specifically, you could be racing about from pillar to post. What would work best is a steady and serene attitude overlaying a growing confidence.

16 SUNDAY   *Moon Age Day 13   Moon Sign Sagittarius*

Friends may be inclined to let you down today, probably at the time you need their support the most. Out of the blue, you might decide to brush up your life somehow and if you look around there are agencies that will give you significant support. Avoid unnecessary family arguments later in the day.

17 MONDAY   *Moon Age Day 14   Moon Sign Sagittarius*

It's time to take things somewhat slower. The lunar low is upon you now, and other planetary trends are already exerting an influence upon you too. There might be a lot to get done but you should address it all slowly and steadily, avoiding any tendency to rush things without good cause.

18 TUESDAY   *Moon Age Day 15   Moon Sign Capricorn*

Outdoor pursuits, especially ones that necessitate travel, are likely to be right up your street this week. There is a chance that you won't easily settle to anything and that your mind will be inclined to wander but at least you won't prove to be remotely boring to those with whom you mix.

19 WEDNESDAY *Moon Age Day 16   Moon Sign Capricorn*

There's no doubt about it, you are in the mood for adventure. It would be advantageous for you to move around and to learn something about other cultures. Sticking to the same old routines won't appeal you at all right now so that even if you can't get away in a physical sense, you are likely to do so in your mind.

20 THURSDAY   *Moon Age Day 17   Moon Sign Capricorn*

Romance could be uppermost in your mind and you will want to prove to someone very special that you are fully committed to them. It might be party time for some Geminis, though the lure of the outdoors still calls you so you won't want to confine yourself for very long at a time.

21 FRIDAY   *Moon Age Day 18   Moon Sign Aquarius*

Your present freewheeling attitude is likely to be a joy to everyone. Gemini can be quite a worrier on occasions but this doesn't appear to be the case at all now. There are decisions that need to be taken with regard to house and home. You will want to think things through, so perhaps right now isn't the best time.

22 SATURDAY   *Moon Age Day 19   Moon Sign Aquarius*

Career developments seem to be your best, and maybe for today your only, area of excellence. In other respects you won't be all that pleased with yourself but this state of affairs is set to alter by tomorrow. It could seem as if practically everything you do at present has to be undertaken twice.

23 SUNDAY   *Moon Age Day 20   Moon Sign Pisces*

You could talk anyone into practically anything at the moment and won't be fazed by any situation at all. With an excess of energy and a great determination to show your mettle, who is there around to stop you? Don't spend all day working or on practical matters because there are very real social rewards on offer.

24 MONDAY   *Moon Age Day 21   Moon Sign Pisces*

Work opportunities can lead to advancement, even if this is something you haven't been expecting. You show yourself to be extremely capable right now and will be coming up with ideas that are certain to get you noticed. Keep up your determination to bring others round to a more sensible frame of mind.

25 TUESDAY
Moon Age Day 22   Moon Sign Pisces

This is a time during which you should be organising your career objectives so that you know better where you are heading, and why. You are not lacking in confidence but you may hesitate over certain decisions if you don't have all the evidence you feel you need to be able to proceed. Take care to avoid procrastination, though.

26 WEDNESDAY
Moon Age Day 23   Moon Sign Aries

Your emotional state of mind isn't all it should be on occasions today. You could find yourself to be slightly irritable, though for reasons you don't really understand. Nevertheless, there are gains to be made, particularly in practical matters. A steady attitude towards life and anything that requires a change now works best.

27 THURSDAY
Moon Age Day 24   Moon Sign Aries

There are plenty of opportunities around now for personal expansion and growth, even if some of them are slightly misplaced at this particular time. Your mind is working overtime and you have all it takes to see your life unfolding for the future. Don't rush your fences though. Slow and steady is best.

28 FRIDAY
Moon Age Day 25   Moon Sign Taurus

Today has trends that indicate you could be slightly less sensitive than usual when it comes to assessing and dealing with others. This is certainly likely to be the case with your life partner and possibly with relatives. Put in that extra bit of effort that counts when it comes to close attachments.

29 SATURDAY
Moon Age Day 26   Moon Sign Taurus

Meeting new friends, moving around and going to exciting locations all are important at the moment. This is the most positive face Gemini can show and one thing it brings is popularity. Since the way others feel about you is important to your self-esteem, you should be high in your own estimation right now.

30 SUNDAY

Moon Age Day 27   Moon Sign Gemini

You need to split your efforts this weekend for the best chance of getting ahead generally. There are times for Gemini when solid concentration counts but this would not particularly interest you right now and so could lead to mistakes. This is an interlude when you really can tackle several jobs at once.

♊ July 2019

1 MONDAY
Moon Age Day 28   Moon Sign Gemini

This is an excellent time for getting new projects underway and also for making gains as a result of ideas you had some time ago. Use the full force of your personality because it's unlikely anyone can resist you at present. People should be only too willing to go along with your ambitious suggestions.

2 TUESDAY
Moon Age Day 0   Moon Sign Gemini

Get an early start today and continue your efforts across all your waking hours. This is important partly because good fortune is on your side but also on account of your tremendous energy. It doesn't matter what sphere of life you are dealing with because you can turn them all to your advantage.

3 WEDNESDAY
Moon Age Day 1   Moon Sign Cancer

Your attention should be focused on your own needs today. Selfishness is far from typical Gemini behaviour but there are times when it is necessary. Nevertheless, you make a good job of entertaining others as you go about it and should make some new friends, almost without any effort at all.

4 THURSDAY
Moon Age Day 2   Moon Sign Cancer

Keeping abreast of everything that happens in your vicinity is quite important now. Although you are keeping up to date with necessary jobs, you still get the impression that there is more and more to do. It is possible that you are panicking unnecessarily. Take the time to stand back and look at matters from a distance to get perspective.

5 FRIDAY
Moon Age Day 3   Moon Sign Leo

Your power to attract just the right sort of people into your life has seldom been more noteworthy than is the case now. Get any jobs you see as being urgent out of the way as quickly as you can. Once you have done so, the time is right to socialise as much as you can. Contacts made at the moment can be important.

6 SATURDAY
Moon Age Day 4   Moon Sign Leo

Along comes a time during which you will want to seek new experiences. All day long your mind is working, even if you find yourself committed to the routines of everyday life. It has to be said that this would be one of the most fortunate periods of the year for Gemini to take a holiday.

7 SUNDAY
Moon Age Day 5   Moon Sign Virgo

Keep life as varied as you can and don't allow yourself to be pushed into a form of drudgery that really isn't your thing at present. They say that variety is the spice of life and that certainly seems to be the case for you now. Long-term plans really are not your present forte, and you live, exclusively, for the moment.

8 MONDAY
☿   *Moon Age Day 6   Moon Sign Virgo*

An extra boost to social trends is now indicated, making this, potentially, one of the best Mondays of the year. The less you plan specifically, the more spontaneous you become and the greater is your sense of enjoyment. Don't take anything too seriously, especially yourself.

9 TUESDAY
☿   *Moon Age Day 7   Moon Sign Libra*

Your mental energies remain strong and this is hardly likely to be a run-of-the-mill sort of Tuesday. For starters, you won't be too keen to sit around and enjoy any good summer weather because you have a desire for movement and activity. You feel the need to keep talking at the moment and you won't be over fussy regarding the people you choose to chat to.

10 WEDNESDAY ☿   *Moon Age Day 8   Moon Sign Libra*

It is almost certain that you will be undertaking more than one task at once today. You can do this thanks to a plethora of positive planetary positions and aspects surrounding you at present. Just remember that you do need to rest sometime. Perhaps some hours to yourself in the evening would be good?

11 THURSDAY ☿   *Moon Age Day 9   Moon Sign Scorpio*

Look out for a period of personal excitement, especially where love and relationships are concerned. You simply will not be held back right now and can break down just about any barrier that gets in your way. With plenty of reassurance coming from the direction to those you trust, even greater possibilities are in view.

12 FRIDAY ☿   *Moon Age Day 10   Moon Sign Scorpio*

Your most successful moments today are those during which you can work closely with people you both trust and like. If you are employed in professional tasks this Friday, then so much the better. Whatever you are doing, make sure that typical Gemini smile is never far from your face.

13 SATURDAY ☿ *Moon Age Day 11   Moon Sign Sagittarius*

With the lunar low now around, you will have all the time you need to review specific elements of your life and to put them into perspective. Although it seems that not everyone has your best interests at heart, take care not to judge too harshly, either today or tomorrow. Your point of view is not neutral under current trends.

14 SUNDAY ☿ *Moon Age Day 12   Moon Sign Sagittarius*

Get as much rest as you can and avoid pushing yourself too much. In one sense, it doesn't matter how hard you work because you simply can't get ahead whilst the Moon is in your opposite zodiac sign. It would be far better to stand and look at certain elements of life from a sensible distance.

15 MONDAY ☿ *Moon Age Day 13   Moon Sign Capricorn*

If you box clever and use some friendly persuasion when you are with colleagues, you might get on better at work as a result. You are perhaps somewhat quieter than would usually be the case though this tends to make you more thoughtful and able to come up with answers that might pass you by in busier moments.

16 TUESDAY ☿ *Moon Age Day 14   Moon Sign Capricorn*

You can be rather impulsive when it comes to speaking your mind right now but there are moments when it would be a definite advantage to hold your tongue. This is particularly true in family conversations or when you are faced with an issue at work. Gemini doesn't need to shout to get its point across.

17 WEDNESDAY ☿ *Moon Age Day 15   Moon Sign Capricorn*

It seems that you will make no more than steady progress towards your chosen professional goals today, but that's all it takes to get ahead. The only potential problem is one of boredom, especially if you are required to do the same things over and over again. Ring the changes when you can.

18 THURSDAY ☿ *Moon Age Day 16   Moon Sign Aquarius*

You need diplomacy and co-operation in equal measure in order to get the very best from wayward family members but this will not prevent you from having fun. The greater your ability to escape routine and to travel, even short distances, the more complete is your sense of enjoyment.

19 FRIDAY ☿ *Moon Age Day 17   Moon Sign Aquarius*

This is a period during which you can make steady progress towards your chosen objectives. You can develop new skills and confidence and won't have any problem at all getting others to go along with your far-reaching ideas. Romance could start to blossom before the day is out.

20 SATURDAY   ☿   *Moon Age Day 18   Moon Sign Pisces*

The things you discover today, whether you are looking for them or not, are going to be of great use to you in the weeks and months ahead. Your natural curiosity is definitely highlighted, leading you to ask numerous questions. How else can you get to know what is going on?

21 SUNDAY   ☿   *Moon Age Day 19   Moon Sign Pisces*

The focus is now on family life and on comfort and security. You may now feel less inclined to travel far and even routine professional commitments could seem to be something of a drag. Don't be too quick to take offence over a certain issue when you know in your heart that none was really intended.

22 MONDAY   ☿   *Moon Age Day 20   Moon Sign Pisces*

You enjoy the company of others today, though more in groups than on a one-to-one basis. This doesn't mean you will have difficulty with personal attachments because you are as committed to your spouse or partner as ever. All the same, you can get a great deal more joy out of foursomes than as a duo.

23 TUESDAY   ☿   *Moon Age Day 21   Moon Sign Aries*

You might have to put up with feeling second best in some situations but remember that a 'feeling' is all it is. It isn't like Gemini to be paranoid as a rule but this could be the case right now. Simply enjoy yourself and don't ask too many questions as to why you are having a good time.

24 WEDNESDAY ☿   *Moon Age Day 22   Moon Sign Aries*

You may have to dig deep in order to get the root of an emotional worry today. If you look hard enough it is possible you will discover, however, that it doesn't really exist at all. Your confidence remains essentially high when you are dealing with practical matters and there isn't much that can hold you back.

25 THURSDAY   ☿   *Moon Age Day 23   Moon Sign Taurus*

Friendship and teamwork are both important factors in the way you are dealing with day-to-day situations today. There is certainly plenty to be done and some of it might get in the way of simply having fun. Actually, there are ways of dealing with life that mean you can work with a smile and even get others to help you.

26 FRIDAY   ☿   *Moon Age Day 24   Moon Sign Taurus*

Your very friendly attitude today makes this a fine time for co-operative ventures of almost any sort. There are gains to be made from simply being in the right place at the right time and since your intuition is so strong at the moment, it should not difficult for you to get ahead in a number of ways.

27 SATURDAY   ☿   *Moon Age Day 25   Moon Sign Taurus*

Don't make any spur of the moment decisions today and be willing to proceed slowly towards your objectives. You will find yourself to be a little more thoughtful and perhaps less inclined to shoot from the hip than is sometimes the case. This interlude comes courtesy of present planetary trends and will not be permanent.

28 SUNDAY   ☿   *Moon Age Day 26   Moon Sign Gemini*

Prepare for some unexpected favours to come your way today. If these achieve nothing else, they could stimulate your faith in human nature. Just about everything in the garden is coming up roses so you can afford to spend more time and money on those projects you know to be important.

29 MONDAY   ☿   *Moon Age Day 27   Moon Sign Gemini*

The lunar high is still with you, promoting a positive attitude and stimulating your desire for knowledge. With silver-tongued eloquence, you won't be held back when it comes to speaking to almost anyone. It isn't out of the question that you could stumble across someone quite famous today.

30 TUESDAY ☿ *Moon Age Day 28 Moon Sign Cancer*

Emotions are all too close to the surface for some Geminis now, but it probably won't do you any good to try to hide them. Most of the people you deal with today are just as intuitive as you are and will see through any sort of disguise. Acting on impulse might be the best approach now.

31 WEDNESDAY ☿ *Moon Age Day 0 Moon Sign Cancer*

Avoid needless disagreements, especially with those on whom you rely a good deal. It could be that you are simply in a fractious frame of mind or maybe you are slightly off-colour. Whatever the reason, you should be able to bite your tongue. Gemini isn't at its best in disagreements of any sort right now.

August

2019

1 THURSDAY

Moon Age Day 1   Moon Sign Leo

Today could not be considered a peak of mental or physical activity, but that is not to suggest you will fail to make any headway. You are likely to be in a thoughtful frame of mind and could be thinking about plans that still lie sometime in the future. You may have a chance to consolidate relationships later in the day.

2 FRIDAY

Moon Age Day 2   Moon Sign Leo

Now there is good incentive and a strengthened desire to push forward. Although not everyone might applaud your thoughts and actions, as long as you can carry even a couple of people with you, your confidence will grow. The naturally persuasive qualities of your zodiac sign are quite noticeable to all at the moment.

3 SATURDAY

Moon Age Day 3   Moon Sign Virgo

This can be a wonderful time for enlivening the social scene. Gemini is right back on form and definitely making an impression when to do so counts most. There may be new incentives to make money, even if some of these remain in the planning stage through what is essentially a practical planning Saturday.

4 SUNDAY

Moon Age Day 4   Moon Sign Virgo

If there are difficulties regarding emotional ties, try to stand back and look at the situation from a distance. Getting too involved in discussions that could so easily turn into disagreements isn't to be recommended. You will do yourself a favour if you keep most of your contact with others light and even superficial for now.

5 MONDAY
Moon Age Day 5   Moon Sign Libra

Getting ahead in life right now is just as much about charm and personality as it is about really knowing what you are doing. You will need to show the true Gemini qualities within you this week. Any chance to get away from the normal routines of the day should be firmly grasped with both hands.

6 TUESDAY
Moon Age Day 6   Moon Sign Libra

There may be someone aiding your rise in life this week and the process begins today. Don't turn away from advice, especially when it comes from people who quite plainly know what they are talking about. Sometime in the afternoon or evening, you could discover something to your advantage regarding money.

7 WEDNESDAY
Moon Age Day 7   Moon Sign Scorpio

There are gains to be made today but some of them come from less than likely directions. With strong social trends prevailing, you are almost certainly making the most of the summer weather to mix with friends and make new acquaintances. Look out for some very striking compliments coming your way.

8 THURSDAY
Moon Age Day 8   Moon Sign Scorpio

This is not a period during which you should be seeking too much in the way of responsibility. Better by far to find enjoyment for yourself and best of all if you could take a break. It appears that old friend of yours, wanderlust, could be paying you a visit at any time now.

9 FRIDAY
Moon Age Day 9   Moon Sign Sagittarius

Plans you have laid down carefully may look as if they are going awry today but you need to keep your nerve and not take any action for a couple of days. Don't be afraid to spend some time relaxing because when the Moon is in your opposite zodiac sign, being somewhat lazy can be seen as part of the package.

10 SATURDAY   *Moon Age Day 10   Moon Sign Sagittarius*

You still won't be making a great deal of headway but the fog is likely to clear somewhat as the day advances. Keep an open mind about the domestic ideas of relatives and don't dismiss any possibilities until you have at least given them fair consideration. There could be a romantic interlude later in the day.

11 SUNDAY   *Moon Age Day 11   Moon Sign Sagittarius*

While your mind is working quickly enough at present, there is a distinct possibility that your body is refusing to keep up. Your power to influence situations may be somewhat diminished, leading you to rely heavily on others. Never mind, you've helped them out often enough in the past.

12 MONDAY   *Moon Age Day 12   Moon Sign Capricorn*

Don't be too influenced by emotional moods and do what you can to keep things ticking along nicely, especially in the career stakes. Love pays a visit sometime soon, which is most noticeable for Geminis who are seeking a new attachment. All those born under the sign of the Twins can expect compliments to come their way.

13 TUESDAY   *Moon Age Day 13   Moon Sign Capricorn*

Places of leisure and entertainment hold some pleasant surprises for you around now. As trends begin to speed up, so you feel more energetic and probably somewhat luckier into the bargain. As August moves on, make the most of the remainder of the summer and get out of doors.

14 WEDNESDAY   *Moon Age Day 14   Moon Sign Aquarius*

Avoid any offers that appear too good to be true. There are times during which you can pick up some genuine bargains, but this really isn't such a period. Your love of luxury shows itself and for the next couple of days, you should indulge yourself if you can, while keeping a close eye on your spending.

15 THURSDAY   *Moon Age Day 15   Moon Sign Aquarius*

A joint financial issue needs looking at very carefully and most probably deserves an intense discussion. That's fine if you are in the mood but the chances are that this is not the case right now. Competing for the attention of loved ones today might mean turning off the television set and throwing away the remote control.

16 FRIDAY   *Moon Age Day 16   Moon Sign Aquarius*

A personal matter might need thinking about fairly seriously today but that is probably because you have been putting it on the shelf of late. Although you may have a tendency to get a little down about things, as long as you listen to the very sound advice that others are offering, all should be well.

17 SATURDAY   *Moon Age Day 17   Moon Sign Pisces*

Be open to new and enlightening experiences that will help to broaden your horizons in every area of life. You have everything you need to progress, even if you can't necessarily recognise this yourself just at the moment. Someone you don't see very often could be making a renewed appearance in your life.

18 SUNDAY   *Moon Age Day 18   Moon Sign Pisces*

You tend to be quite idealistic right now, perhaps a little too much so for your own good. Realise that in some ways life is simply the way it is and understand your limitations. That doesn't mean settling for second-best, merely being realistic. What you can alter you can come to terms with.

19 MONDAY   *Moon Age Day 19   Moon Sign Aries*

Simplify your daily routines in order to create an environment that is favourable to your future success. Concentrate and to pick your priorities carefully, sidestepping some of the dross of life so that you can get where you would most want to be. Romance is especially well accented now.

20 TUESDAY
Moon Age Day 20   Moon Sign Aries

Trying to please others could be something of a thankless task at the moment. The fact is that you cannot please all the people all the time, especially when you need to be happy with your lot, too. Compromises are called for and nobody in the whole of the zodiac is better at them than you are.

21 WEDNESDAY
Moon Age Day 21   Moon Sign Aries

Keep your ears open today because what you learn from others could prove to be very important as far as your own life is concerned. It could be that some extra responsibility you are taking on around this time proves to someone in authority just how capable you really are.

22 THURSDAY
Moon Age Day 22   Moon Sign Taurus

You may find opportunities to enjoy social contacts and to get the very best out of situations that may once have worried you a little. It's amazing just how much confidence you have at present but don't forget the build-up to this state of affairs has taken time and your present attitude should not be taken for granted.

23 FRIDAY
Moon Age Day 23   Moon Sign Taurus

You should be feeling quite happy and contented at the moment, which of course is the very best way for Gemini to be. There are things around to entertain you, and you may get the chance to pit your wits against friends and those who are arriving brand new into your life. It should be easy to make a good impression.

24 SATURDAY
Moon Age Day 24   Moon Sign Gemini

High spirits prevail and it appears that you have everything you need to make the best possible impression on a variety of different people. Confident to stick up for your point of view, don't be surprised if you fail to raise reaction in those around you. It may well be that people are unwilling to cross swords with you for the moment.

25 SUNDAY
Moon Age Day 25   Moon Sign Gemini

Getting your own way is so easy now that you might not bother trying. Certainly, you are enjoying the limelight in one way or another, perhaps because you are taking part in some sort of public event. You should have good reason to feel proud of yourself, but even more so of younger family members or the children of friends.

26 MONDAY
Moon Age Day 26   Moon Sign Cancer

A more challenging time is on the way and you relish the opportunities it brings. Instead of sitting and listening to what others are saying about any situation, you now decide to join in and speak your mind. Any new health regime commenced at this time is likely to endure.

27 TUESDAY
Moon Age Day 27   Moon Sign Cancer

Social and romantic relationships need to be looked at again and possibly revived in some way. That extra bit of effort you are capable of putting in can be of tremendous importance and will lead to some startling results in a day or so. By this evening you will probably be ready to let your hair down.

28 WEDNESDAY
Moon Age Day 28   Moon Sign Leo

Inspiring ideas come along from a wealth of different directions today, leading to potential excitement and a new way of looking at old situations. Trends favour travel, so Geminis who have chosen to take any sort of holiday or short break at this time will have chosen very wisely indeed.

29 THURSDAY
Moon Age Day 29   Moon Sign Leo

Teamwork and co-operation are what counts at present and this period can be all the better for mixing with others. Don't try to go it alone too much because this simply isn't necessary. Someone you don't see often could be coming back into your life on a much more regular basis.

30 FRIDAY
Moon Age Day 0   Moon Sign Virgo

You easily express charm and grace at the moment. This is the true face of Gemini and is one that everyone loves. Your confidence is never far from the surface and although you find committing yourself to future projects is not so easy at the moment, you are lightening the load of many people with whom you make contact.

31 SATURDAY
Moon Age Day 1   Moon Sign Virgo

It may go without saying that you need to put certain issues in the past and to continue on your way with a greater sense of commitment, but it is worth registering this fact all the same. Keep telling yourself that what lies ahead is going to be bigger, better and brighter than what you are leaving behind.

♍ II September 2019

1 SUNDAY
Moon Age Day 2   Moon Sign Libra

Make sure you are open to new experiences because there are likely to be a number of them turning up in the coming week. From the very start, you should have plenty of vitality. What really stands out is your ability to communicate with almost anyone. However, you may not be too good today with routine or tedious jobs.

2 MONDAY
Moon Age Day 3   Moon Sign Libra

There are matters to be faced head on today, some of which you might prefer not to address. It's best to be brave and plunge in headfirst; that way you get things sorted out very early in the day. Later on, you can turn your attention towards having fun, something that definitely does appeal.

3 TUESDAY
Moon Age Day 4   Moon Sign Scorpio

This is hardly the best time for jobs that demand absolute concentration, so Geminis who are not at work today are better off than those who are. Instead of trying to work against the odds, take some hours to yourself if you can. If at all possible today you should only do those things that have a definite appeal.

4 WEDNESDAY
Moon Age Day 5   Moon Sign Scorpio

This would not be a good time to hold back any strong feelings. Speak your mind and trust that those listening understand your genuine motivations. It isn't usually too difficult for you to get your message across and there are planetary influences around now that make the job that much easier.

5 THURSDAY
Moon Age Day 6   Moon Sign Scorpio

You thrive on challenges today, especially professional ones. There are influences around in the sky now that show you to be like a terrier with a rag once you have made up your mind and adopted a specific course of action. No amount of persuasion will change your mind in this, though in many other matters you remain flexible.

6 FRIDAY
Moon Age Day 7   Moon Sign Sagittarius

Before today is out you might have to admit that you do not have all the answers to every conceivable problem. Listen to the sound advice that comes from people you trust as this is certainly not the right day this month to go it alone. Fortunately, in other ways the lunar low should fail to impact you too much.

7 SATURDAY
Moon Age Day 8   Moon Sign Sagittarius

Despite the continued presence of this month's lunar low, you remain in a very positive frame of mind and so therefore might not even have too much cause to notice it. Continue to go for what you want in life generally, though realise that when you shoot for the Moon you might only reach the stars! Shun too many rules and regulations if you can.

8 SUNDAY
Moon Age Day 9   Moon Sign Capricorn

Today should be an excellent time to make new contacts. Look out for the chance to socialise on a bigger scene than might normally be the case and don't turn down any chance to get on your glad rags and have fun. Some interesting news may come along via the telephone or maybe a text message.

9 MONDAY
Moon Age Day 10   Moon Sign Capricorn

This would be an excellent time to be thinking up new ideas, or even adopting some of those of your friends. On so many occasions you can help others realise their full potential but right now you may get the chance to help yourself at the same time.

10 TUESDAY   *Moon Age Day 11   Moon Sign Aquarius*

You need to be amongst familiar faces at the moment because it is from this direction that most of the positive aspects of life will spring. Gemini is good with strangers as a rule but it is somewhat doubtful at present whether you are likely to make much headway when faced with people you haven't met before.

11 WEDNESDAY   *Moon Age Day 12   Moon Sign Aquarius*

It looks as though everyone wants to be in your good books today, so this is as good a time as any to get ahead. Life is filled with contrasts at the moment, all of which help to demonstrate the many directions that are open to you. Career matters slip into the background as you get into socialising mode.

12 THURSDAY   *Moon Age Day 13   Moon Sign Aquarius*

The input that comes from others today may prove to be extremely rewarding and offer you a host of new possibilities, or provide the ideas for them at least. Money matters need careful handling but there are people around who are in a good position to offer sound, impartial advice if you listen to them.

13 FRIDAY   *Moon Age Day 14   Moon Sign Pisces*

The pace of everyday life quickens again, bringing you face to face with a few of your own limitations. Most of these are brought about simply because you are trying to do too many things at the same time. Halve the jobs and then concentrate more on the remainder. The result should be a greater degree of success.

14 SATURDAY   *Moon Age Day 15   Moon Sign Pisces*

You can't rely on luck or believe everything you hear today. Although it is your natural way to trust everyone, it has to be said that there are people around at the moment who definitely don't have your best interests at heart. Trends suggest that some Geminis will now be embarking on a new keep fit campaign.

15 SUNDAY   *Moon Age Day 16   Moon Sign Aries*

It appears that you will be restless to try something new today, but are not entirely sure about what it should be. Your confidence is really going off the scale and as a result you could be inclined to take too many chances. Be patient, if only for a short while and exercise caution before you act on anything now.

16 MONDAY   *Moon Age Day 17   Moon Sign Aries*

When it comes to projects you have had on the go for some time, this is the period during which you gather the fruit. You are a hard worker and also willing to wait for your rewards but there don't seem to have been all that many of late. However, things are changing now and in some ways so are you.

17 TUESDAY   *Moon Age Day 18   Moon Sign Aries*

There is just a possibility that you will be viewing some matters in a slightly less than sensible way. This is particularly likely to be the case when it comes to practical considerations that also have an emotional content. Trends favour seeking out the advice of an impartial observer for support.

18 WEDNESDAY   *Moon Age Day 19   Moon Sign Taurus*

You may now reap some very real material benefits, and feel a great sense of certainty regarding the future. If you have had some worries on your mind, now is the time to put them behind you and to cast your mind forward. Relatives and friends alike should prove to be ultra-supportive today.

19 THURSDAY   *Moon Age Day 20   Moon Sign Taurus*

Social and romantic encounters may well have some extra sparkle today and there isn't much doubt that you shine out when in company. Although your commitment to hard work might not be what it usually is, you do know very well how to have a good time, something that a few of your friends might have forgotten for now.

20 FRIDAY · Moon Age Day 21 · Moon Sign Gemini

This is the best time imaginable to take independent decisions and to make up your mind regarding medium and long-term projects. Most important of all is the way you are dealing with the various facets of your life. Love and romance might continue to be at the top of your agenda.

21 SATURDAY · Moon Age Day 22 · Moon Sign Gemini

A sprinkling of good luck may improve your feelings about life in general. You are very much inclined to trust to your own judgement, which is sound at present. Concentrate on having a good time, even when you are undertaking jobs that might sometimes prove to be either distracting or difficult.

22 SUNDAY · Moon Age Day 23 · Moon Sign Gemini

You want to organise yourself today and to focus on issues you see as being extremely important for the future. It might seem as though very few people are offering the sort of emotional or personal support you would wish this Sunday but the truth might actually be that you are looking in the wrong direction.

23 MONDAY · Moon Age Day 24 · Moon Sign Cancer

The start of this week is not going to be all bells and whistles. On the contrary, you would do much better if you simply decided to take your time and to plan carefully for the short-term future. No matter how hard you try right now, all that is going to happen is that you will have to start again later.

24 TUESDAY · Moon Age Day 25 · Moon Sign Cancer

A more dynamic and determined Gemini is now evident and making a great impression on everyone. You should now find it easy to get your own way, not because you are exerting too much influence but simply because you have the right sort of manner to make the world sit up and take notice.

25 WEDNESDAY   *Moon Age Day 26   Moon Sign Leo*

This would be a particularly good time to broaden your horizons in just about any way you can. Don't be too inclined to sit in the shadows, even when you are dealing with issues you profess not to understand. Learning on your feet is part of being born under the very adaptable sign of Gemini.

26 THURSDAY   *Moon Age Day 27   Moon Sign Leo*

When it comes to personal ambitions, this is the time to lay them all on the line and to go for gold. There will never be a better series of general trends around than those that have a bearing on your now. Don't allow yourself to be held back by people who really don't know anything about you or your life.

27 FRIDAY   *Moon Age Day 28   Moon Sign Virgo*

You enjoy harmony and co-operation, especially in your professional life. That's what you are looking for right now but if it's hard to find, concentrate on home and enjoy a little romance instead. You might discover something about someone you thought you knew well and this could have a positive bearing on the way you view them.

28 SATURDAY   *Moon Age Day 0   Moon Sign Virgo*

You might spend at least part of this Saturday looking at your finances. There are definitely material gains to be made if you concentrate on monetary on matters closely. Being able to focus well comes with the astrological territory at the moment and you have a good ability to see well into the future.

29 SUNDAY   *Moon Age Day 1   Moon Sign Libra*

Today can be filled with romantic promise if that is what you are looking for. However, there are also strong social trends about and you should have the ability to see your way forward better than may have been the case for quite a while. In general terms, this has to be a high spot for Gemini.

30 MONDAY
Moon Age Day 2   Moon Sign Libra

Your imagination is stimulated at every turn and you prove to be extremely intuitive right now. This is why you cannot afford to take anything for granted, especially when your brain is sending you some important messages. Trust your instincts. Romantic overtures are also likely at any time this week.

October 2019

1 TUESDAY
Moon Age Day 3   Moon Sign Scorpio

Emotional issues and the way you view them are inclined to dominate personal relationships at present while in reality practical matters should be taking centre stage. If you can, defuse issues before they take on any real significance and avoid getting involved in discussions you know could be contentious.

2 WEDNESDAY
Moon Age Day 4   Moon Sign Scorpio

You are in a good mood to look for professional developments, which might mean that a simple friendship takes something of a back seat at this stage of the week, especially if you are so busy with other things that you neglect it somewhat. Exercise some caution in financial matters.

3 THURSDAY
Moon Age Day 5   Moon Sign Sagittarius

Not all plans are working out strictly as you might have wished today and there is a good deal of thinking on your feet to be done. The behaviour of others can give you food for thought, though since you are extremely intuitive at present, you should be able to work out their reasoning.

4 FRIDAY
Moon Age Day 6   Moon Sign Sagittarius

Let go of the reins for a while and allow the world to do more or less what it wants. Once again, the lunar low is not an incredible affair but it can take the wind out of your sails to some extent. Avoid confronting family members or cornering anyone into an argument you don't really want yourself.

5 SATURDAY
Moon Age Day 7   Moon Sign Capricorn

It should prove to be the case that your social life is on a roll this weekend, even if closer attachments are still somewhat more remote than usual. Part of the potential problem stems from temporary planetary trends that make it harder for you to verbalise your innermost feelings.

6 SUNDAY
Moon Age Day 8   Moon Sign Capricorn

What really sets you apart right now is your ability to speak in public situations, and to elicit the necessary response from others. This is nothing particularly new but is a quality much enhanced by present planetary trends. In a business sense, it is possible that new ideas are coming along at all stages today.

7 MONDAY
Moon Age Day 9   Moon Sign Capricorn

You are ready for almost any challenge life can throw at you, plus a few you invent for yourself. Take care not to set out to attack imaginary enemies or you could lead yourself into difficulties. If you haven't enough to do there are people close by who would welcome a helping hand.

8 TUESDAY
Moon Age Day 10   Moon Sign Aquarius

In money matters, your present ability to think quickly is going to prove extremely useful. Although you are unlikely to be gambling in the generally accepted sense of the word, you are willing to take a chance that could lead to greater monetary strength further down the line. Make time to enjoy yourself later in the day.

9 WEDNESDAY
Moon Age Day 11   Moon Sign Aquarius

There may not be time to do everything you have planned today, but you will be determined to at least have a try. Your confidence remains essentially high, particularly when you are dealing with subject matter that is familiar to you. Your potential to create is especially strong and shows itself through all facets of life.

10 THURSDAY
Moon Age Day 12   Moon Sign Pisces

The challenge today is to keep one step ahead of the competition. This is as true at work as it is in more social or sporting situations. Not everyone you know will be adept at expressing either their opinions or wishes today. This could lead to a good deal of second-guessing as far as you are concerned.

11 FRIDAY
Moon Age Day 13   Moon Sign Pisces

Your chart reveals some highlights in love and romance, which might come as something of a shock to a few Geminis who have placed such considerations firmly on the back burner during the last couple of weeks. If you feel at all lethargic today, the secret is to pitch in early in the day to boost your sense of achievement.

12 SATURDAY
Moon Age Day 14   Moon Sign Pisces

Current planetary trends have the ability to bring out the best in you and they help to make life stable and people around you supportive. You should feel generally comfortable at home this Saturday and might not have that need for movement that has been so much a part of your mood across the last few weeks.

13 SUNDAY
Moon Age Day 15   Moon Sign Aries

Trends move on and today a degree of restlessness may begin to pervade your life as October moves on. You need something different to do and perhaps some alternative people to share the situation with you. Sunday can be interesting but it all really depends on just how much effort you are willing to put in.

14 MONDAY
Moon Age Day 16   Moon Sign Aries

Financial consolidation is on your mind and you could be looking at the family finances very closely indeed. Don't be fooled into making any purchase that you know to be flippant or unnecessary. Keep a cool head in a minor crisis and you will soon be laughing at the whole situation.

15 TUESDAY   *Moon Age Day 17   Moon Sign Taurus*

Though there is little doubt that you have a big ego at the moment, you retain your usual ability to turn on the charm whenever necessary. This is fortunate because you need to let those around you know how much you care about them and also reassure family members of your continued practical and emotional support.

16 WEDNESDAY   *Moon Age Day 18   Moon Sign Taurus*

You continue to be fond of the good life and there isn't much doubt that luxury in one form or another is going to play an important part in your day today. It may be necessary to rearrange your schedules somewhat, possibly to accommodate others. Take note that putting yourself out in this way may have hidden benefits.

17 THURSDAY   *Moon Age Day 19   Moon Sign Taurus*

Life can be quite hectic, but should still be eventful and exciting. Things you learn today, even in casual conversations, may turn out to be very important in the fullness of time. Don't set too much store by routines because these are almost certain to bore you between now and the weekend.

18 FRIDAY   *Moon Age Day 20   Moon Sign Gemini*

The lunar high does much to redress a few balances now and finds you more grounded in your attitude. Discussions with others should be less strained and you have strong diplomatic skills, which are not always a strength for your zodiac sign. When it comes to money, you can afford to chance your arm at the moment.

19 SATURDAY   *Moon Age Day 21   Moon Sign Gemini*

Now you can speed ahead and make more genuine progress than might have been possible for some days, despite any adjustments that have taken place in your life. The difference now is that you are more considerate in your attitude and you are integrating relationships and practical matters much better.

20 SUNDAY
Moon Age Day 22   Moon Sign Cancer

Don't insist on everything running absolutely smoothly because this is not likely to be the case today. You might have to put up with second-best in one or two situations but your ability to plan for the future has rarely been better. Give yourself credit for a certain series of successes in personal matters.

21 MONDAY
Moon Age Day 23   Moon Sign Cancer

Beware of a slight prima donna approach to some situations. This will only occur in matters about which you know a great deal and where others are trying to muscle in on you. All the same, yours is the most conciliatory of natures now and this state of affairs should not change today.

22 TUESDAY
Moon Age Day 24   Moon Sign Leo

Any form of public relations exercise that is undertaken right now is almost certain to go well. You are on top form when it comes to getting on with others and your powers of communication have rarely been stronger. Don't take no for an answer when you know exactly what you are talking about.

23 WEDNESDAY
Moon Age Day 25   Moon Sign Leo

Material affairs look less stable than usual today, so try to defer decisions and instead turn your mind towards personal matters. Finding the time to let your partner know how important they are to you would be ideal today. Those Geminis who are looking for love should turn up the light of their passion now.

24 THURSDAY
Moon Age Day 26   Moon Sign Virgo

Today should be favourable for intellectual endeavours and for learning something new about yourself or life. Friends should be especially attentive around now and can offer some very sensible and timely advice. Don't be too willing to cut back financially just because of a couple of worries.

25 FRIDAY
Moon Age Day 27   Moon Sign Virgo

There might be a slight sense of urgency about something today, even if you can't quite put your finger on what it might be. In all probability the present astrological trends are making you fidgety, though without any just cause. Try to relax and to enjoy what this rather positive sort of Friday has to offer.

26 SATURDAY
Moon Age Day 28   Moon Sign Libra

Your self-confidence is strong so don't be afraid to commit yourself to what promises to be a wild and wonderful sort of weekend. Don't be constrained and certainly avoid staying around home all day. You need fresh air and stimulation, which you can enjoy in the company of someone very special.

27 SUNDAY
Moon Age Day 0   Moon Sign Libra

You can easily express your ideas at the moment and that's what counts if you want to get on in most situations. People who don't often figure in your life may be putting in guest appearances at present and it is not out of the question that you could meet someone who has been something of an idol in the past.

28 MONDAY
Moon Age Day 1   Moon Sign Scorpio

You should be pretty much in tune with your financial goals and general objectives right now and since you spend quite a lot of your time worrying about money, this should turn out to be a very positive state of affairs. Avoid looking back too much today because it won't really help at the moment.

29 TUESDAY
Moon Age Day 2   Moon Sign Scorpio

Though your influence over practical matters may not be quite as notable as you would wish, you can still make a sort of progress. If you are forced to take some time out, enjoy it. This is a day to go with the trends, rather than trying to fight against them. In any case, everything will look different by tomorrow.

30 WEDNESDAY   *Moon Age Day 3   Moon Sign Sagittarius*

Your engaging personality is usually one of your best assets but rarely more so than now. It can win people round and also allow you to take small liberties that might normally be out of the question. Almost everyone loves you at present, a state of affairs that increases your confidence.

31 THURSDAY   *Moon Age Day 4   Moon Sign Sagittarius*

Emotions run quite close to the surface throughout most of today and you will have to be quite sensible in the way your view personal situations. It would be all too easy to take offence when none was intended and that could lead to a slight sense of anger or even failure. Look at situations carefully as it is possible that you are not being realistic.

November

2019

1 FRIDAY
☿ *Moon Age Day 5   Moon Sign Sagittarius*

Today is a time for thinking about recent proposals and for following them to their logical conclusion. If you have recently embarked on something that could only really be called a labour of love, you may be about to discover that it can also be profitable. Aim to spend part of your Friday with family members.

2 SATURDAY
☿ *Moon Age Day 6   Moon Sign Capricorn*

The further you are able to go today, the better you will feel. This is true in terms of journeys you might choose to take, but also with regard to issues that you are likely to push beyond previous limits. Don't allow anyone or anything to hold you back during this most important interlude.

3 SUNDAY
☿ *Moon Age Day 7   Moon Sign Capricorn*

Professional matters can be a real labour of love today, which is just as well because they are not offering too much in the way of financial remuneration. Be patient, better monetary times are to come, but they are not here yet. All the same, be certain that you check your lottery ticket carefully if you have bought one today.

4 MONDAY
☿ *Moon Age Day 8   Moon Sign Aquarius*

Don't listen to the tall tales of others today and at the same time take care not to spread any gossip yourself. If you need to know something, it would be far better to check out the details for yourself. You are quite creative now and might be in the mood to turn out a delicious meal.

142

5 TUESDAY   ☿   *Moon Age Day 9*   *Moon Sign Aquarius*

As far as personal and emotional security are concerned, you should find yourself well looked after today. You should be in a charming mood and well organised at the moment – with just the right attitude necessary to get on well in life. You also exude a sort of wisdom that others will recognise.

6 WEDNESDAY   ☿   *Moon Age Day 10*   *Moon Sign Pisces*

In practical matters, you need to keep your eye on the ball. This is not a time to diversify too much and concentration is all-important. If you feel that family members are not taking their own responsibilities quite as seriously as they should, this might be the right time to gently let them know.

7 THURSDAY   ☿   *Moon Age Day 11*   *Moon Sign Pisces*

Things that are happening at home help to redress the balance at work, where you are likely to be extremely active. Use some of your spare hours to quite simply have a rest and don't take on any more tasks than are strictly necessary at this time. Avoid getting on the wrong side of someone who is quite influential.

8 FRIDAY   ☿   *Moon Age Day 12*   *Moon Sign Pisces*

A combination of leisure and romance ought to appeal today in those moments when you are not busy working. If you want to avoid becoming bored with routines, it would be sensible to deliberately make alterations to your regimes. There is little to worry about at the moment, though probably a shortage of excitement.

9 SATURDAY   ☿   *Moon Age Day 13*   *Moon Sign Aries*

Now you find yourself well able to get your ideas across to others and to make the very best of impressions on the world at large. It is as if you have suddenly heard the starter's gun because you race ahead, particularly in practical matters. Romantically speaking, you ought to let someone know how you feel.

10 SUNDAY ☿ *Moon Age Day 14   Moon Sign Aries*

You can definitely benefit from getting out and about today. Being held in the same place all the time won't appeal to you, and you should not be afraid to state your need for personal freedom to those around you. Most of the people you meet today understand your point of view and ought to offer support.

11 MONDAY ☿ *Moon Age Day 15   Moon Sign Taurus*

It looks as though you will be taking an 'easy come, easy go' attitude towards money at present. This is probably just as well because, with Christmas close at hand, you are likely to be spending more than usual. Take some time out to listen to your partner and understand what really makes them tick at present.

12 TUESDAY ☿ *Moon Age Day 16   Moon Sign Taurus*

Minor complications are apt to arise regarding work. Perhaps people are difficult to deal with, or you don't quite understand exactly what is expected of you. No matter what the problem might be, you should keep a cool head and use the same diplomatic skills you have recently shown.

13 WEDNESDAY ☿ *Moon Age Day 17   Moon Sign Taurus*

It is clear that you are less socially inclined today, probably because the Moon is in your solar twelfth house. This makes you a great deal quieter than of late and more contemplative too. You may have to let close friends, as well as your partner, know that you are not sulking about anything.

14 THURSDAY ☿ *Moon Age Day 18   Moon Sign Gemini*

You can expect to be the centre of attention today, which is why it would be sensible to line up in your mind all those things you would wish others to do for you. It isn't selfish to take advantage of your popularity and in any case most of the people you encounter will be more than happy to oblige.

15 FRIDAY ☿ *Moon Age Day 19* *Moon Sign Gemini*

Colleagues and friends will find you to be talkative, inquisitive and extremely friendly at the moment. Your level of general good luck is high, so you can afford to go an odd step further than would usually be the case. Love and romance may lie in wait around the corner for Geminis who are actively seeking either.

16 SATURDAY ☿ *Moon Age Day 20* *Moon Sign Cancer*

There are influences around today that should be supportive in a financial sense. Don't be too quick to make judgements about others now and be willing to wait and see in most situations. Someone in the family or your immediate friendship circle could be quite surprising around this time.

17 SUNDAY ☿ *Moon Age Day 21* *Moon Sign Cancer*

The bright lights of the social world have a specific attraction for you at this time and you can't wait to get out there and wow everyone. This is not a good time to be thwarted in your plans and it is quite certain that you are now happiest when you are the centre of attention.

18 MONDAY ☿ *Moon Age Day 22* *Moon Sign Leo*

The pressure to get things done could be evident now, particularly at work. Try not to be pushed into anything because in the end you need to choose for yourself. There is probably more time than you think and plenty of chance to check a few details with people who are in the know.

19 TUESDAY ☿ *Moon Age Day 23* *Moon Sign Leo*

This is likely to be a far more favourable day with regard to finances and you might just find that there is money around you didn't expect. This is the start of what should be a solid, stable period and whilst it might not be quite as exciting as some of the summer months, it does have its appeal.

20 WEDNESDAY ☿ *Moon Age Day 24   Moon Sign Leo*

Your general awareness of situations surrounding you increases and you turn detective in a number of ways. It is important to look below the surface of apparent happenings and in doing so you will show the world just how perceptive Gemini can be. The events unfolding around you could bring a little more excitement.

21 THURSDAY *Moon Age Day 25   Moon Sign Virgo*

You may get a great deal from general developments in the practical side of life. Even tasks you don't usually care for should be easy to cope with today and you have tremendous affection for family members and close friends. There is likely to be something especially warm about today.

22 FRIDAY *Moon Age Day 26   Moon Sign Virgo*

Your generally happy outlook brings you popularity today and indeed for much of the coming week. This isn't all that unusual for your zodiac sign but the tendency is much increased. It should be easy to prove just how genuine you are and nobody is likely to doubt your integrity at present.

23 SATURDAY *Moon Age Day 27   Moon Sign Libra*

Some last minute but important information could lead to a change of plan. Fortunately, you were born under one of the most adaptable signs of the zodiac so altering things isn't difficult for you and doesn't create too many stresses. Your creative potential is especially good and should assist you to also make changes at home.

24 SUNDAY *Moon Age Day 28   Moon Sign Libra*

What really attracts you to others right now is their intellect. You are happiest when you are mixing with people who are thinkers and the more refined qualities within your nature are also now on display. In social situations you have the chance to shine and you may even surprise yourself.

25 MONDAY   *Moon Age Day 29   Moon Sign Scorpio*

Today is helpful when it comes to getting more from your work in a financial sense. Perhaps you are being offered different sorts of responsibilities but it is up to you to make sure that you don't lose out as a result. Use a little cheek and take any chance that is offered to ask for what you want.

26 TUESDAY   *Moon Age Day 0   Moon Sign Scorpio*

Extend yourself in social situations and understand that is now possible for you to mix business with pleasure. Make the most of romantic offers and wow the world with your style. Although the middle of the working week might seem a strange time to shine, it's quite possible for you.

27 WEDNESDAY   *Moon Age Day 1   Moon Sign Sagittarius*

You will be taking life steadily now. The lunar low does little to curb your enthusiasm, though it can prevent you from taking too much in the way of direct action. With Christmas only about a month away, you might be spending time making lists and getting your social life sorted out ahead of the holiday period.

28 THURSDAY   *Moon Age Day 2   Moon Sign Sagittarius*

Be as sensitive to the moods of others as you can be today and show just how caring the average Gemini is. Your concern for the underdog is very noticeable right now and will continue to be so for some days. Romance can play a part in your day, especially if you are in the market for a new attachment.

29 FRIDAY   *Moon Age Day 3   Moon Sign Capricorn*

There could be some slight tension about, most noticeably between you and someone with whom you work. Be prepared to show that famous Gemini flexibility. Actually, if you are very careful you can get your own way but without others realising that this is the case. You remain confident, but in a low-key way.

30 SATURDAY   *Moon Age Day 4   Moon Sign Capricorn*

Some confusion could attend personal matters, maybe because you don't quite understand the needs and wishes of those around you to the extent you normally would. This might mean that you have to second-guess the way others are likely to behave, which isn't going to be all that easy.

♊ December
2019

1 SUNDAY ☿ *Moon Age Day 5   Moon Sign Virgo*

Family issues can be dealt with in a flash under current trends, but it isn't this side of life that appeals the most this Sunday. On the contrary, you are turning your attention outside of home and probably gaining a great deal by looking further afield. Aware of what is in the news, you also feel the need to discuss almost everything.

2 MONDAY ☿ *Moon Age Day 6   Moon Sign Libra*

There can be fruitful encounters with a number of different individuals today, some of whom are offering the sort of information that is both timely and useful. Where love and romance are concerned, it is not difficult to find the right words to sweep someone off their feet.

3 TUESDAY ☿ *Moon Age Day 7   Moon Sign Libra*

Any sense of urgency on your part today could well be misplaced. The fact is that you are getting on rather well with most aspects of life, even if some of them are not coming good quite as quickly as you might wish. Stay aware of the needs you know family members have of you, especially those of your partner.

4 WEDNESDAY ☿ *Moon Age Day 8   Moon Sign Scorpio*

The main area of fulfilment today should be your family. Getting on positively in terms of your career is slightly more difficult, though any problems here are likely to be little more than a hiccup. Socially, it appears that the festive season has started already for Gemini.

5 THURSDAY ☿ *Moon Age Day 9   Moon Sign Scorpio*

Your fun-loving nature is stimulated by present planetary trends and that means the joker inside you is showing at almost every turn. Try not to hold back in any situation, simply because you doubt the reaction of colleagues. You have things to say, and the world should be quite willing to lend an ear.

6 FRIDAY ☿ *Moon Age Day 10   Moon Sign Scorpio*

You can look forward to an influx of bright new ideas today and should expect to be on the receiving end of a positive audience. Your usual ways of relaxing might not fit the bill at present and it is entirely possible that you will be looking for new ways to pep up your social hours, particularly this evening.

7 SATURDAY *Moon Age Day 11   Moon Sign Sagittarius*

You would move heaven and earth to make someone you care about happy, but even that might not be enough. Accept that you can't be held responsible for everyone all of the time. As long as you bear this in mind, and offer assistance when you can, you are doing everything that could be expected of a decent human being.

8 SUNDAY *Moon Age Day 12   Moon Sign Sagittarius*

Don't get too concerned about any slight difficulties in terms of money today. As long as you have your eye on your finances at all times, these trends should only indicate a temporary glitch. Make tasks you have to undertake part of a logical process, starting at the beginning and working steadily through to their completion.

9 MONDAY *Moon Age Day 13   Moon Sign Capricorn*

This is likely to be a freewheeling period during which you will be happy to break with convention and to do what comes naturally to you. There are very few people around at the moment who see the future any better than you do yourself so you may not feel the need to seek the advice of others.

YOUR DAILY GUIDE TO DECEMBER 2019

10 TUESDAY   *Moon Age Day 14   Moon Sign Capricorn*

The more romantic side of your nature is on display today and the present position of the Moon adds to your ability to get on well with your partner. If you don't have one, this might be a good time to look around because it's almost certain that someone has their eyes on you at present!

11 WEDNESDAY   *Moon Age Day 15   Moon Sign Aquarius*

This is a good way to face the middle of the working week: with the Moon in your sign and in a generally good mood about life. Don't be held back by anyone standing in your way at the moment but move them aside and follow through with plans that have been hatching in your mind for quite some time now.

12 THURSDAY   *Moon Age Day 16   Moon Sign Aquarius*

When slightly risky situations arise now you can afford to back your intuition, which is extremely strong at the moment. Gemini is fond of taking the odd little chances and the ones around at present are calculated. Money matters should be better and you are keeping the necessities of Christmas well in view.

13 FRIDAY   *Moon Age Day 17   Moon Sign Aquarius*

You can bring out the best in others now and it ought to be obvious from the moment you get out of bed that there is little to hold you back. Your communication skills are now second to none and you won't have any problem making the sort of impression that ensures you are high on everyone's Christmas list.

14 SATURDAY   *Moon Age Day 18   Moon Sign Pisces*

Be open to a variety of views and allow yourself to be drawn out of a slightly self-indulgent phase that has descended. Make contact with anyone you need to in order to get the last practical tasks over and done with before the holidays swallow some of your efforts. Friends should be very supportive.

15 SUNDAY
Moon Age Day 19   Moon Sign Pisces

You may hear some promising news relating to your short-term plans and aims. That alone makes this a time to act swiftly and not a period during which you can afford to procrastinate. The best way to succeed in most situations is to deal with matters yourself, which you do whilst others are still thinking about them.

16 MONDAY
Moon Age Day 20   Moon Sign Pisces

You are likely to be in most people's good books now, so if there is something you really want, this is probably the best time of all to be asking for it. Controlling your expenditure might be awkward, which is hardly surprising at this time of year, but there are some bargains around if you look carefully.

17 TUESDAY
Moon Age Day 21   Moon Sign Aries

This might be the last chance to get new and invigorating plans off the ground before Christmas comes along. It's true that not everyone will accept your word as law, but you should have the chance to prove yourself to a great extent. Someone you don't see very often might be putting in an appearance quite soon.

18 WEDNESDAY
Moon Age Day 22   Moon Sign Aries

Your confidence holds you in good stead when you need it the most but for the majority of today you simply go with the flow. There isn't really anything that will hold you back but no specific journey is likely to seem very important, physical or mental. Gemini is happy to enjoy some luxury instead now.

19 THURSDAY
Moon Age Day 23   Moon Sign Taurus

Today ought to bring you closer to achieving a specific objective. This might be as a result of some early gift you received but is just as likely to owe something to a journey you are going to take today. If you are at work today it should be possible to get on the good side of people who matter.

20 FRIDAY
Moon Age Day 24   Moon Sign Taurus

Optimism is your best gift at the best of times but certainly turns out to be so right now. Not everyone will be on your side however, particularly when it comes to medium-term plans and practical matters. Trust your own judgement, which is especially sound at the moment, no matter what others believe.

21 SATURDAY
Moon Age Day 25   Moon Sign Gemini

Some of your actions today could be rather reckless, but as long as you realise this is a possibility, you should also be able to rein yourself in somewhat. The problem stems from the fact that present astrological trends make it feel stimulating to take risks. Remember that others have to watch you and that they might be concerned.

22 SUNDAY
Moon Age Day 26   Moon Sign Gemini

Although your hearth and home may continue to be your main focus, you are likely to be going through a rather indulgent phase. It seems as though you need to feel quite secure and that little luxuries enhance that security. All thoughts of Christmas could be out of the window for today.

23 MONDAY
Moon Age Day 27   Moon Sign Cancer

Work and all practical matters receive a definite boost now and it won't be at all hard for you to get what you want in a material sense. Don't be too quick to believe everything you hear, especially where your personal or family life is concerned. If you have to sign any documents, read the small print.

24 TUESDAY
Moon Age Day 28   Moon Sign Cancer

Forget high expectations for this Christmas Eve. Whilst the lunar low is around it would be sensible to simply bide your time. Get a decent rest before the holidays begin. What might suit you the best right now is to spend some hours with loved ones.

25 WEDNESDAY
Moon Age Day 29   Moon Sign Leo

Enjoy Christmas Day, but be aware that the planets could throw you one or two setbacks. These become less likely if you are not too over-confident in your approach. Leave any suggestions for new plans or ideas until tomorrow, by which time there's a good chance you will have amended your strategy.

26 THURSDAY
Moon Age Day 0   Moon Sign Leo

This is certainly likely to be a very positive time when it comes to pleasing family members and friends alike. You can consider this to be 'your' day during the Christmas break and a time when you can choose to do more or less what suits you. This might include spending at least some time alone.

27 FRIDAY
Moon Age Day 1   Moon Sign Virgo

The most interesting times today come when you are swapping stories and jokes with people you feel comfortable around. Don't take anything too seriously at present and be quite willing to see the really funny side of life, which shows itself time and again throughout the day.

28 SATURDAY
Moon Age Day 2   Moon Sign Virgo

In pursuit of your goals and objectives today, you might encounter one or two stumbling blocks. Don't allow these to hold you back because there is no reason at all for them to do so. You have enough energy and sufficient determination to ensure that you win through in the end.

29 SUNDAY
Moon Age Day 3   Moon Sign Libra

A little soul-searching might be in order at this stage of the holidays. It is possible you took certain actions last week that you now wish you had not. It might be impossible to replay the situation but there are ways you can explain yourself. The evening should be good for romantic proposals.

30 MONDAY
Moon Age Day 4   Moon Sign Libra

This is a particularly good time for entertaining at home and for attending to those little details that make all the difference in any situation. You should be able to make others extremely happy and won't be likely to feel jealous in personal relationships, even if you are being pushed in some way.

31 TUESDAY
Moon Age Day 5   Moon Sign Libra

Entertaining people at home ought to prove to be immensely satisfying at the moment, but you may discover that there isn't quite as much scope for romance as you might have wished. If the right words to please your partner elude you for the moment, keep things simple and enjoy the festivities.

RISING SIGNS FOR GEMINI

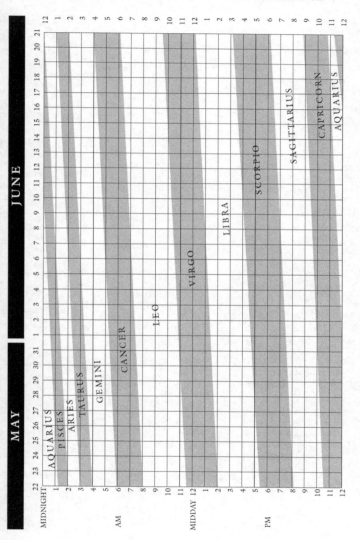

157

THE ZODIAC, PLANETS AND CORRESPONDENCES

The Earth revolves around the Sun once every calendar year, so when viewed from Earth, the Sun appears in a different part of the sky as the year progresses. In astrology, these parts of the sky are divided into the signs of the zodiac and so this means that the signs are organised in a circle. The circle begins with Aries and ends with Pisces.

Taking the zodiac sign as a starting point, astrologers then work with all the positions of planets, stars and many other factors to calculate horoscopes and birth charts and tell us what the stars have in store for us.

The table below shows the planets and Elements for each of the signs of the zodiac. Each sign belongs to one of the four Elements: Fire, Air, Earth or Water. Fire signs are creative and enthusiastic; Air signs are mentally active and thoughtful; Earth signs are constructive and practical; Water signs are emotional and have strong feelings.

It also shows the metals and gemstones associated with, or corresponding with, each sign. The correspondence is made when a metal or stone possesses properties that are held in common with a particular sign of the zodiac.

Finally, the table shows the opposite of each star sign – this is the opposite sign in the astrological circle.

Placed	Sign	Symbol	Element	Planet	Metal	Stone	Opposite
1	Aries	Ram	Fire	Mars	Iron	Bloodstone	Libra
2	Taurus	Bull	Earth	Venus	Copper	Sapphire	Scorpio
3	Gemini	Twins	Air	Mercury	Mercury	Tiger's Eye	Sagittarius
4	Cancer	Crab	Water	Moon	Silver	Pearl	Capricorn
5	Leo	Lion	Fire	Sun	Gold	Ruby	Aquarius
6	Virgo	Maiden	Earth	Mercury	Mercury	Sardonyx	Pisces
7	Libra	Scales	Air	Venus	Copper	Sapphire	Aries
8	Scorpio	Scorpion	Water	Pluto	Plutonium	Jasper	Taurus
9	Sagittarius	Archer	Fire	Jupiter	Tin	Topaz	Gemini
10	Capricorn	Goat	Earth	Saturn	Lead	Black Onyx	Cancer
11	Aquarius	Waterbearer	Air	Uranus	Uranium	Amethyst	Leo
12	Pisces	Fishes	Water	Neptune	Tin	Moonstone	Virgo